Steve,

You're fabulous!

# folding time ™

# what thought leaders are saying about folding time

With the demands of business, time is always a challenge. Neen's recommendations for being productive and smart about how you use your time are gems for all professionals. Her advice not only is practical and immediate; most importantly her techniques work. When you take action and implement Neen's expertise, you will have positive results improving your attention on how you use every minute of your day.

**Stacey Hanke** CEO Stacey Hanke Inc.

If there is one thing I need, it's more time! As a small business owner with 11 employees I have a never-ending to-do list that keeps me working 16-18 hours a day. I am a wife, I am a mother, and I am hyper-connected, which allows me to get work done, anywhere, anytime… and that is one of my biggest problems!

Neen's book has given me a new perspective on time and my use of it. I have begun making different decisions, becoming more intentional with my time and actually getting more done! This book is not for the person looking for a few time management tips. This book is for the overworked, over scheduled person who packs 2 weeks of work into each day!

**Gina Schreck** President, SocialKNX

All of us are being asked to do more with less, but there are still only 24 hours in each day. Some people are masters of productivity, while others always feel the stress of too many deadlines. When you learn to "Fold Time" you stop allowing the outside world to control your future. Neen James does a great job in helping all of us find that allusive thing called "Focus".

**Thom Singer** The Conference Catalyst

# what thought leaders are saying about folding time

As a leader you are not only responsible for your own productivity, but for helping those on your team be as productive as possible, and not just at work, but at home as well. Neen made this book easy to digest and implement the strategies immediately. It's not just a book of theory or unrealistic tips for someone who keeps laminated checklists for their family members. Neen provides nuggets of wisdom and then weaves in the insights from other experts that it is like 10 books rolled into one.

The fact that Neen shares strategies for maintaining priorities in your life to achieve more, is refreshing. This book provides people with the knowledge needed to take control of their lives and their destiny. No more whining. It's up to you to become more efficient, more productive and more successful. You will find this in our required reading library for the 1500+ team members at HomeAdvisor!

**Kirk Schreck** COO, Home Advisor

In this book, Neen James teaches you the best ways and techniques to manage your time. In this busy world we live in have half the time to do twice as much. Neen breaks down the process and helps you truly see the importance of your time management. She gives so many tips that not only help with time, but would benefit you on the job, managing the home, and everything in between. I took a couple of days and implemented a few of Neen's tips. I can't believe the difference I saw in my time while following just a few of them. If you are a boss, employee, parent, homemaker, or and adult for that matter, you need to read this book!

**Chad Hymas** Owner Hymas Communications

# what thought leaders are saying about folding time

I'm very impressed with Neen's ability to deliver enduring results.  Neen has the ability to motivate leaders and young professionals to expand their knowledge to develop and deploy new "Super Productive" concepts.  Neen's teaching style is energetic, thoughtful and will make you want to take your skills to the next level - and immediately!

This tool will do the same. It will force you to rethink unproductive habits and turn them into capabilities  that yields continuous, high-impact results that endure!

**Andrea A. Agnew** Executive Director,
Workforce Diversity & Inclusion- Comcast

*Folding Time* is not just another book on productivity.  It is a book about focus, integration and improving performance.  It's a book about choices,  the deliberate choices we can make on how to manage and spend our time and the potential rewards that can come along as a result.  If you are a corporate leader, the practical tips Neen James shares in *Folding Time* are ideal strategies to bring to your team.  Entrepreneurs and solo business owners trapped in the old workaholic stereotype can find insights to help them work smarter and reap the benefits  that a more flexible, self-imposed schedule offers and perhaps remember again why they decided to go it alone.

Throw out the out-dated productivity manuals and work-life balance books that never worked  and reclaim some space on your shelf, then read *Folding Time* and reclaim some space in your life.

**Karen Roy** Principal Ardgillan Group

## what thought leaders are saying about folding time

It's not about doing everything; it's about doing what matters! If you are looking to regain control of your over-worked, over-tired and over- committed life; so you can focus on what matters and who matters, then *Folding Time* will give you practical everyday tools you can implement immediately. *Folding Time* is easy to read, easy to understand and brilliantly on target!

**Kim Woodworth** Regional Vice President - Comcast Spotlight

Library of Congress Cataloguing-in-Publication Data is available.

ISBN 978-0-9769258-3-5

Cover and book design by Jeff Braun, TriFecta Creative

These books are available at special discount when purchased in bulk for premiums and sales promotions as well as for fund-raising or educational use.  Special editions or book excerpts also can be created to specification.  For details, contact the Sales Director below.

Neen James Communications
PO Box 1764
Doylestown, PA 18901 USA
www.neenjames.com

Printed in the United States of America.

First Printing June 2013.

with love to Maddie and Ava

# contents

# acknowledgments

Writing a book is an adventure — one that you can become obsessed with. The book is a constant companion always with you; always challenging you, always stretching you to think beyond any way you've ever thought before and always on your mind.

To write acknowledgements of those who have assisted in this adventure is risky, as I fear I may forget someone. So if you have shared the productivity adventure with me as an audience member, maybe we have chatted on Facebook, connected on Twitter or you have been part of our mentoring program, this is for you. A huge thank you to my clients who constantly astound me with the amazing results they achieve by applying these ideas to their professional and personal lives.

There are five amazing women in my life in the USA who have gone above and beyond what you could ever expect from a friendship. Each of them has impacted my life in more ways than they will ever know. Our weekly conversations by phone, Skype, Twitter and Facebook — and especially our accountability emails — have kept me encouraged and on track and constantly challenged me to be more, do more and expect more of myself. I adore you all and there are no words to express how much I love and appreciate you – **Meg Kristel**, **Stacey Hanke**, **Kim Huggins**, **Karen Roy** and **Gina Schreck** – this one is for you!

When first becoming a speaker I was exposed to one of the best speakers on the planet. For six months I begged him to mentor me (he constantly refused) until I finally wore him down. A year spent being mentored by him is like drinking from a fire hose, and each time you wonder if you can possibly take anymore he surprises you again with more brilliance. When my adventure took me overseas, his friendship and guidance was always there. More recently we have joined forces again and I am delighted to be part of the movement he founded all those years ago, the Thought Leaders Global community. Thank you, **Matt Church**, for your role in my journey, for your guidance with this book and the impact you have in the world.

Family is a funny thing. As an Aussie living in the USA, I have two families, one in Australia and one in the USA. My dearest American friends here are also my family. Both are equally important to me and this project could not have been completed without their love, encouragement and support.

To my mum and dad, brothers and sisters, your love across the miles is ever present – thank you.

My fabulous **Jen Sellan**, the coolest friend in the whole wide world, our regular (and sometimes at hideous and unglamorous times), Skype chats mean the world to me.

Everyone knows I could never achieve what I do without my Maria. **Maria Novey**, often called the Queen of Neen, and one of the most loyal, committed people I have ever met. Thank you for protecting my time and my sanity while I chose to write this book in such tight timeframes. Thank you for negotiating all the logistics of the project and giving me the freedom to create while you held the fort.

There is no greater influence on my life than my honey that I worship and adore. With over 24+ years of marriage, great adventures, amazing memories, even keeping track of the word count – **Andy** you are my forever, I love you.

If you have read all the way to the bottom of this acknowledgements page … thanks for sticking it out with me. Thank you to you the reader for investing your money — and more importantly your time — to invest in this Folding Time adventure with me.

Let's take this journey together, let's guide each other and then you can guide someone else to Fold Time. Good luck on your journey. Sending you virtual Aussie cuddles and champagne kisses! Cheers!

Neen James, 2013

folding time™

**MORE?** It's perhaps the single most important idea of our time. It's got to be one of the top 3 issues for business in North America, the United Kingdom and other highly developed nations. If Self Actualization was the idea of the last decade then Being Productive is the idea for the next!

# foreword

**We all have to be able to do more with less in the future!**

Talented individuals will soon find that their safe jobs are moved off shore, while office workers see colleagues 'moved on' as budgetary constraints put downwards pressure on the workforce.

Creative professionals who cannot produce to deadline will see their competitive advantage eroded by the flattened globalized market place. Overnight, while you sleep an alternate Creative is working through your night to deliver on the brief.

**Matt Church**
Founder of Thought Leaders Global

Not to put too fine a point on it, but its really is the key to future success for the human race. The principles of waste impact not only on time but on resources. We need to be more resourceful to survive as a race into the future and beyond.

We can talk about cause and effect or even rant and rave about how unfair this may be, or who is to blame, but the bottom line is those who adapt to the new world of getting things done faster will succeed.

They are going to need some semi-magical super powers to juggle the conflicting, horizontal To Do lists that assail the modern professional.

**In short, they need to be able to Fold Time!**

There is so much to love and highlight in this book. I reckon the greatest compliment though is the generous bounty of concise, confident tips, on almost any page.

You could open this book to a different page every day and get a new idea for getting on with it. Perhaps that's the time folded way to read it?

Neen has for as long as I've known her (and that's a long while) been obsessed with finding out strategies and tactics that help others to punch above their weight and over deliver on their own personal expectations.

**Read fast, learn deep and start folding time.**

- **Folding time is about achieving twice as much in half the time.**

- **Be accountable – choose how you invest your time.**

- **Be engaged – focus your attention on what you are doing.**

- **Be leveraged – systemize everything.**

- **You don't have time to do everything, only time to do what matters.**

- **Multitasking doesn't work.**

- **Stop wasting time.**

- **Filter your decisions to impact your time.**

- **Determine the best flow to maximize time.**

- **Increase your time investment in the highest return activities.**

- **Bring personal integrity to all situations.**

- **Make the impact you were born to make.**

"Folding time is about being accountable for our time, engaging our attention and leveraging our energy."

- Neen James

The law of exponential growth occurs when the growth rate of the value of a mathematical function is proportional to the function's current value. An example often cited is when folding a piece of paper (the similar thickness of pages used in the Bible). When you fold it 45 times you will reach the moon. Learning to Fold Time will accelerate everything you do – shoot for the moon!

There are so many books, blogs and apps available on productivity. These outline time management, effectiveness, efficiency, getting organized and tools and resources to help you get more done. It seems everyone is an expert on this topic; there are many opinions on productivity … so why write another book on this topic? Simple: the old way of managing time doesn't work anymore!

In one of our previously published books, *Secrets of Super-Productivity: How to Achieve Amazing Things in Your Work Life*, we share that **time management is out the window: We can't manage time … time is going to happen … whether you like it or not!**

Technology has changed the pace and way in which we work. There is no such thing as a 9am–5pm job anymore where you can go, work, leave and keep your work and personal life separate.

Now more than ever before, we are being asked to do more with less resources, shorter timeframes, tighter budgets, reduced headcount –and all the while delivering exceptional service and quality for our clients.

We can't manage time – we need to Fold Time.

**Folding time is about achieving twice the results in half the time.**
Have you ever attended a time management-training program? What do they tell you to do? Make a list and prioritize the list, e.g., A, B, C … but does C ever really get done? Of course not!

Is it possible to spend more time managing our to-do list than actually doing our to-do list? I wonder ... are you one of those people who write things on a to-do list ... just so you can cross it off? We need to ask ourselves: are the right things making it onto our to-do lists?

The old way of managing time doesn't work in our fast paced, ever changing, dynamic environment. It's not about managing time; it's about Folding Time.

Folding Time is taking half as long to achieve twice the results. It is consciously choosing to invest half the time but expecting twice the results. We are being asked to do more with less. The solution: learn to Fold Time.

## Be accountable

Be accountable for how you invest your time and choose to stop wasting time. Remember: you get 1440 minutes per day to invest. How will you spend yours?

## Be engaged

To effectively Fold Time we need to focus our attention and be fully engaged. Multi-tasking doesn't work. To Fold Time, choose to be fully present, to listen intently and to give your undivided attention to the task or person.

## Be Leveraged

In everything ask yourself, "Can I systemize or leverage this?" Is there a template you can create? One of the people I admire is Matt Church, founder of Thought Leaders Global, and he says, "Think once, sell often." Love this idea of total leverage!

## Increase investment

When you are accountable for time and you put your energy into activities that are giving you the greatest return, you increase your investment in people, projects and results.

### Increase integrity

When you invest time and truly engage in conversations, meetings and presentations your personal integrity increases. You listen deeply, respond appropriately and build credibility.

### Increase impact

When you engage your attention and leverage your energy you make a greater impact in your organization, community and with the people you truly care about because you are aligning your values and beliefs to make a greater impact on the planet.

### Manage flow

To Fold Time also requires you to constantly assess your workflow. Are you working efficiently? Are you working on the most effective activities? Are you systemizing and leveraging all opportunities?

### Apply filter

To Fold Time effectively means you need to apply a filter to your choices. Your daily, hourly, minute decisions need to be filtered through the correct objectives and goals. A question to constantly ask yourself ... Is this the best use of my time right now?

Folding Time is about being accountable for your time, engaging your attention and leveraging your energy. When you combine these vital success filters you are able to ensure that every project you invest in you can approach with full integrity and you will have an impact on the planet.

## We don't have time to do everything; we only have time to do what matters.

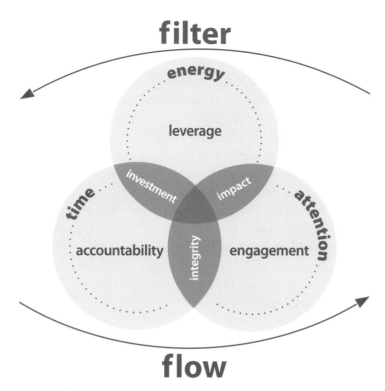

When writing one of our books, *Secrets of Super-Productivity*, the focus was on how to manage time, focus attention and leverage energy – those principles are still important today! In fact, they are essential ingredients in the *Folding Time* model. However, with our global economy changing, technology advancing and lifestyles evolving it has to be more than that!

*Secrets of Super-Productivity* focused on how to manage yourself, your work, your position and your career. This valuable resource (of course, I am biased) is a practical, how-to, bullet point, easy to read, designed for people who don't have time to read book.

This book, *Folding Time*, is the evolution of super-productivity. It is also conscious of the reader who doesn't have time (or desire, or the attention span) to read every chapter. So we have made it easy for you!  Each chapter has a summary at the beginning called **Accelerate**! If you are pressed for time or prefer the executive summary, just read **Accelerate** – that's all you need! For those of you who want to get more specific, keep reading. How does that sound to you?

Many years ago I became involved in a community that is changing the planet. Thought Leaders Global **www.thoughtleadersglobal.com** is an education company that helps clever people become commercially smart. Using your expertise, we help people capture, package and deliver your thought leadership for commercial success. This community is full of brilliant minds changing the planet through their work and projects. Brilliant minds, while creative, also need discipline and focus to get more done. Throughout this book you will meet some of the brilliant minds I admire, and they will share their thought leadership with you through the interviews we did with them.

As a thought leader in the area of productivity, I became obsessed with helping clever people get more done so they could create more significant moments in their lives.  Some of the clients we have worked with have seen increases in their personal productivity ranging from 30–80% -and one public relations firm we worked with increased their book of business by 100%! What impresses me about our clients is that they learn to get more done at work so they can go home and deepen their relationships with those they love, pursue passions they had only ever dreamed of, take vacations they have never thought possible – all because they learned how to Fold Time.

This book will be like taking a multi-vitamin, full of ingredients that will help you feel more productive at work and at home.

What makes this book unique is the global perspective (being an Aussie, living in the USA and speaking around the globe) combined with the knowledge that it is more than time management – it is about Folding Time to be productive: being accountable, fully engaged and leveraging every opportunity.

We know you will enjoy the practical, implementable strategies for everyday activities – so you can personally can get more done, spend more time with people you love, and remember why you do what you do!

A quick overview of the book for you (in case you want to skip to the chapter that is most interesting to you):

**Accountable** – This chapter focuses on how you can be accountable for time by taking responsibility for how you invest in decisions that reflect your personal integrity.

**Engagement** – This chapter will share how you can invest your attention, and then engage the attention of others and maximize your impact.

**Leverage** – This chapter focuses on leveraging your energy by investing in activities that give you the greatest impact at work, at home and in your community.

**Flow** – This chapter shares how systems create freedom so that when you templatize your life you are in a constant state of flow and your 'work flow' feels more productive.

**Filter** – This chapter challenges you to make strategic decisions so you can filter choices that will maximize your time, attention and energy.

Often it is people who are already good time managers that buy books like this one. If that is you – awesome! If not, you might have bought this book because you desperately want to reduce your sense of overwhelm and change your chaos to calm – welcome! Regardless of the situation you find yourself in, we hope you enjoy scanning the pages and finding ideas that you can apply every day!

After all, don't we all want to be able to get more done so we can spend more time with the people we really care about?  Let's take this Folding Time journey together – welcome aboard!

your thoughts

- Technology has changed the pace at which we work.

- We want to get home earlier.

- We need to spend more time with those we love.

- Increase your sense of completion.

- Get clear on focused activity.

- Implement systems to help make better choices around time.

- Increase your sense of contribution.

- Remove conflict in our roles.

- Remove feelings of inadequacy.

- Eliminate distractions.

- Feel more energized.

- Learn to say no ... nicely.

- Release your sense of control.

- Manage procrastination.

"The bottom line is those who adapt to the new world of getting things done faster will succeed."

- Matt Church

Why do we need to Fold Time?

Why doesn't time management work?

Why do we feel exhausted all the time?

Why do we work on vacations?

Why do we get sick once we take time off?

There are many reasons we need to Fold Time:
- We are being asked to do more work with less resources.
- We feel like there is never enough time.
- We are exhausted by a constant state of busy.
- We are 'busy' but not productive.
- The pace at which we work has changed.
- We are constantly in meetings and wonder when we will get our 'real work' done.
- Traditional roles at work and home don't exist anymore.
- There is no work-life balance.
- Communication options have changed and multiplied.
- We have so many projects we don't know where to focus first.
- Our global economy has affected employment significantly.
- Headcount is reduced in corporations and people are not being replaced.
- Team members left after downsizing are expected to pick up the workload of others.
- Lead times have shortened in many industries and lengthened in others.
- We are communicating face to face, electronically and online … the rules have changed.
- We can't complete anything due to lack of focus.
- … And we are exhausted!

The **benefits** of **Folding Time** include:

**Getting you home earlier** – Spending countless hours at the office is not a productive use of time. Some cultures have a 'be seen' mentality where leadership wants to see you in your office or cube – definitely not productive. True leaders know the measurement of an individual's success is measuring outcomes and project completion, not hours sitting at a workstation.

While in the oil industry, we had a boss who wrote down the time people entered and left their workspaces. He wasn't interested in outcomes; he only wanted to see you at your desk. He didn't realize some people were playing the card game Solitaire on their computer – they were looking 'busy' but not being productive! The old mentality needs to shift. Time at work doesn't equal productivity.

If you are working longer than everyone else, taking work home on weekends and constantly checking your email, chances are you might be stuck in a productivity trap. Maybe your way of doing things isn't working. It's time for a shift.

Folding Time will get you home earlier through smart work choices while you are in the office. It means learning skills like productive language (we talk about that more in chapter five).

**Spend more time with those you love** – Isn't that why we work? Don't most of us want to create a lifestyle for the people we care about? When you question why you work as hard as you do, is it because you want to be able to fund a certain lifestyle? That's one of my reasons, and often the most common one we hear from clients in all industries. Long hours, crazy deadlines, endless emails – all things we tolerate because we know that each payment to our bank account was earned, we worked hard for it so we can share it with others.

Folding Time is essential to allow you to **filter your choices**. You can change your workflow to free-up time spent working and invest more time with those you care about.

**Your sense of completion** – When we have a massive to-do list or many things floating around in our brains, it's hard to feel productive. A sense of completion also equals a sense of calm. Engaging in conversations and holding yourself accountable to how you invest time ensures you increase your execution, and that helps fuel completion. Do you feel great when you get something done that you have wanted to do for ages or that you have been procrastinating on? Use that momentum to achieve even more.

**Get clear on focused activity** – We often find working with our clients that their to-do list is long but not correct. It is easy to fill our days with busy work and things we think 'should' be done. Here's a challenge to you: grab your to-do list and check it out. Is there any activity on your list that could be done by someone else? Is there an activity on your list that if you didn't do it … there would be no consequences? Is there anything on your to-do list that you do from habit, not necessity? It is scary to think how much time we invest in activities that don't help us achieve our goals. **Folding Time helps you get clear**.

**Implement systems to make your best choices around time** – Systems create freedom! If you can systemize and templatize your everyday – your time will be well invested, and you free up your brain space for more creative and productive use. When you can create templates and systems you **think once, use often.** This is an essential skill in repurposing. **Folding Time helps you create systems** to increase leverage and accelerate results.

**Sense of contribution** – We all want to feel valued at home and at work. When you see projects complete, new business won, proposals accepted – whatever your measurement – you understand how your everyday activity contributes. **Folding Time increases your contribution.**

**Remove conflict in your roles** – We wear many hats! As a busy woman, I am a wife, business owner, daughter, sister, aunty, board member, accountability partner, Godmother, neighbor, friend … the list is endless. Your list of roles is huge, too. (Especially for all those parents out there that also adds chauffeur, coach, PTA member, counselor, and fixer-upper…) Each day we are challenged to fulfill these roles and responsibilities to those around us. When you focus on achieving the activities that have the highest impact for the roles you fill in life you will be Folding Time.

**Remove feelings of inadequacy** – I often think it is lucky that people can't read the bubbles outside my head. Just like in cartoons, we have thought bubbles that float around us. Thankfully, mind reading technology hasn't been invented … yet! Many of our clients share that they aren't sure if they are 'enough' – if they are doing enough, sharing enough, giving enough attention. They are not alone. We all wonder if we have the right skills, the right training, the right mindset, and the right amount of time to get it all done. When you apply the principles of Folding Time you can reduce this weird sense of insecurity we carry with us.

**Eliminate distractions** – Now more than ever before people can communicate with us in multiple modes. We have verbal, phone, email, text messages, instant message, social media, video presence – and the list continues. We can get our news from TV, radio, print media, online, mobile devices – and the list continues. We can invest time online through web browsing and social media. While we may not be able to totally eliminate distractions, we can manage them. Did you know there are now even apps created to help you block out distraction – a fun one is *Think*. This app blocks out distractions on your computer. Folding Time can limit your focus time in increments so you can double your results.

**Feel more energized** – Have you ever experienced a time when you were so focused on the completion of a project you were loving that time disappeared? You were so into it that you didn't even look at the time! That feeling of being energized by the task or project you are working on is super-productive. When you are working on things that are aligned with you and your values, you will feel more energized!

**Learn how to say no nicely** – Why is it that this word is so difficult for some … and easy for others? There are several reason why no is unacceptable: it could be you were raised in an area that word wasn't acceptable; it could be that you feel you are being impolite by saying no; it could also be that you are wanting to please everyone, so you are reluctant to say no and risk hurting someone's feelings. **Folding Time allows you to be clear about the things you want to say yes to**, and this makes it easier to say no to the others.

**Release your sense of control** – We all want control – admit it! Many of us want to feel more in control because when we are living in chaos it creates emotions we don't enjoy.  If you recognize that you can't do everything all the time, you can let go of the need to be in complete control.

**Manage procrastination** – We all do it, some more than others.  In all the research we did on the topic of procrastination across major universities and papers published online it seemed we found much of the world procrastinates; many of us use it as an excuse for not getting things done.

Piers Steel, a professor of psychology at the University of Calgary in Canada, conducted a significant research study on procrastination in 2007. According to Steel, 20-26% of adults are chronic procrastinators – and as many as 95% are occasional procrastinators (apparently students have a high chronic procrastination rate).

Procrastination is seen as a psychological problem, rather than a time management style.  Most authors on this subject divide the world into procrastinators versus non-procrastinators.  I disagree because everyone procrastinates! There is no such thing as a non-procrastinator.

Procrastination can be paralyzing for a small percentage for the population who really struggle with this. Folding Time allows you to focus your energy and attention on the right things and keeps accountability high for completion.

There are many reasons cited for procrastination, among them (in no particular order):
- ◀ Low self-esteem.
- ◀ Low motivation
  (for various reasons: dislike of task, not considering task as important).
- ◀ Pursuit of instant gratification from other activities.
- ◀ Lack of self-control or self-discipline.
- ◀ Martyr complex.
- ◀ Stubbornness/manipulation.
- ◀ Indecision.
- ◀ Intimidated/overwhelmed by task.
- ◀ Don't understand task/don't know how to accomplish task.
- ◀ Coping mechanism.

Procrastination is an excuse – stop now, choose to Fold Time instead.

Folding Time through leveraging your energy and focusing your attention will give a **greater sense of achievement** on a daily basis; that's why Folding Time is essential for you to master today.

Folding Time is essential to allow you to filter your choices. You can change your workflow to free-up time spent working and invest more time with those you care about.

- **Productivity is more essential now that our lives are so busy.**

- **We need to achieve twice as much with half the amount of resources, sometimes with people with half the experience.**

- **Fix attention poverty with abundance attention.**

- **Focus on the content of your character and the character of your content.**

- **Social media requires us to be more connected.**

- **People seek thought leaders ... not thought repeaters.**

# "The value of an idea lies in the using of it."

- Thomas A. Edison

Productivity is not a new concept; it just seems more essential given our busy lives.

You might occasionally hear people reminisce about the 'good old days' of life before email. There are some people in the workplace who remember when faxes were introduced to the environment ... then along came email, telecommuting, and technology in general. All of these technologies were supposed to be time saving and allow us more 'free time'. Did you know that when the personal computer was invented, one of the goals was to allow people to have more vacation time because systems and processes would be automated?

Why it is now, more than ever before, important to Fold Time? We are all being asked to achieve twice as much with half the time, half the resources and sometimes with people with half the experience.

The global economy has changed, emerging technologies have impacted our everyday activities, and the world feels like it has become smaller. Expectations for our workflow and the projects and deliverables have increased from our leaders and also from our own expectations of ourselves. Technology has forever changed our world and our work, and now we need much tighter guidelines for work boundaries so we can enjoy both personal and recovery time.

People are exhausted by the amount of information available. It is not the information age; it is the age of over-information! People want to have information condensed into manageable bite sized pieces. We crave tweets for their simplicity and brevity.

## Why is Folding Time now important?
Illnesses like heart disease, diabetes and other stress related illnesses are on the rise.

People are not investing in recovery time even though they live their lives connected 24/7. In the USA many companies expect that when you take vacation you will still check in to your email and dial in to teleconferences so you can stay on top of your role while you are supposedly relaxing. This is not a productive operating principle, and human resource departments are being flooded with complaints of burned out, unhappy workers as a result.

As a leader, your responsibility is to help your team understand the fundamentals of how to Fold Time so they can get more done during their work hours – so they can go home and get on with what energizes them.

## Fix attention poverty

Do you have attention poverty? I know I do … more than I am proud to admit in public, but don't tell anyone.

In his book *Free*, Chris Anderson posed the question, "Does multi-tasking just slice the same attention (our attention) more finely?" He quotes social scientist Herbert Simon, who says, "A wealth of information creates a poverty of attention." That Herbert was super smart, if you ask me.

To reduce attention poverty we need to choose abundant attention – focusing our attention and energy on the person in front of us or the task at hand.

## We need an etiquette revolution.

Today's fast paced world demands differentiation between etiquette of technology and social media etiquette.

It's not old irrelevant etiquette; it's an etiquette revolution.

In the 1970's, platform shoes hit the fashion scene. These shoes and their fabulous designs were one of the most memorable fashion statements of the era. As these shoes have reentered fashion over the years, they have evolved and become a staple of many women's shoe wardrobes.

Do you remember those bell-bottom jeans from the same era? I always giggle when see photos of them and yet – the bootleg jeans we all now wear are the evolution of the bell-bottom jeans.

Emily Post, born in 1872, wrote the rules of etiquette in her book *Etiquette in Society, in Business, in Politics and at Home* (more commonly referenced as simply *Etiquette*) first published in 1922 – she was right back then and many of her guidelines are relevant for today.

June Cleaver (an iconic character in American television history) wore pearls and fabulous shoes to clean her house! Seriously … what woman today does that?

Just as fashion has evolved, so has social media, and we need to ensure we understand the etiquette revolution.

I have heard, "If you suck in real life you will suck online."

It is the evolution of formal to the familiar. We have established personal brands and become more accessible to a global community.

People want to interact with those who are fun, authentic and familiar. People want social sharing.

Social media gives everyone a voice, a right to be heard, a platform to share opinions. We need to be aware that this accessibility of information also requires us to be even more diligent with Folding Time. We need to avoid wasting time and engage in conversations with a different level of frequency.

We need to start forgiving text speak and spelling errors in email and focus on message and context. People demand social sharing now.

We need to focus on the content of our character and the character of our content.

It used to be that media was controlled by traditional journalists; now the media seek their news sources through Twitter and online communities.

**People seek thought leaders** in their area of expertise, **not thought repeaters.**

Folding Time is essential now to achieve twice as effective communication in half the time.

- Increase productivity by managing your time, attention and energy.

- Be efficient and effective.

- Be systemized and functional.

- Be leveraged.

- Build engagement.

- Focus on the right activities.

- Focus on strategy.

- Get aligned with your values and beliefs.

- Discover your personal productivity style.

- Are you a planner or a crammer?

- Are you a morning bird or a night owl?

- Work in your most productive time zone for accelerated results.

- Leverage team styles to maximize productivity.

"You don't have time to do everything, only time to do what matters."

- Neen James

**Get more done; become massively productive.**

If you really want to Fold Time you must understand the need to take action. You can't just theorize about all the ways you could do something – you have to be able to execute, implement, just do it!

Over 12 years ago, I partnered with founder of Thought Leaders Global, Matt Church, and created the following matrix as a literature review of all the productivity principles available. When you develop an understanding of each of these productivity strategies and use them to help you you will definitely get more done! This is featured in the great book *Thought Leaders* by Matt Church, Scott Stein and Michael Henderson and is reprinted here for your enjoyment.

## Productivity Matrix

|  | you | someone | teams |
|---|---|---|---|
| **energy** | **Leveraged** make more of it | **Engaged** get into it | **Aligned** one for all |
| **attention** | **Effective** do what matters | **Functional** know the roles | **Strategic** one for all |
| **time** | **Efficient** get across it | **Systemized** step it through | **Active** get on with it |

The model is organized into rows and columns. The first column with **leveraged, effective** and **efficient** is all about how you work personally. The second column with **engaged, functional** and **systemized** is all about how you help a team of people get things done. The third column with **aligned, strategic** and **active** is all about how you engage a community of people to be productive.

The rows also have a frame of reference. The first row with **leveraged, engaged** and **aligned** is how you manage energy. The second row with **effective, functional** and **strategic** is all about how you manage attention and focus. The bottom row with **efficient, systemized** and **active** contains the three ways you manage scarce resources (such as time) efficiently.

You will notice how this productivity matrix has influenced the Folding Time model.

## The evolution of your personal productivity:

### Be efficient

Efficient people are able to get their heads around all the details and elements that need to be done.

- ◀ Take notes in meetings.
- ◀ Learn how to mind map an issue.
- ◀ Create minutes.
- ◀ Set agendas.

### Be effective

Once you know the detail, you have to manage your attention so that you pay attention to those things that will reap the highest return. It is about focusing on the things that matter most and doing them first.

- ◀ Do the important task first.
- ◀ Know your important goals.
- ◀ Manage interruptions so you don't have to split your attention across multiple tasks.
- ◀ Be willing to say no to the little things so you can say yes to the big things.

### Be leveraged

Each task you work on with a small amount of extra effort can reap more benefit than simply the task you are completing. Look at what you are doing with a view to other projects and tasks.

- Repurpose your ideas and reuse them whenever you can.
- Take time to set things up so that you can access them in the future.
- Learn to tag, store and recall everything you do.
- Blend responsibilities whenever possible so you can kill two birds at the same time.

### Get systemized

Systems are the key to making the repetitive tasks in your life and those of your team get done. Systems also save time in the long term.

- Build systems into anything repetitive.
- Write procedures manuals.
- Run induction and training.
- Create habitual ways of doing things with your team members.

### Be functional

Functionality is about people being clear about what their job is and what it is they are meant to do. It is also about you letting go of controlling everything.

- Make sure people know what their job description is.
- Hold consistent accountability conversations with the team.
- Stay out of others' responsibilities.
- Communicate the impact of people not doing their job.

## Build engagement

When people want to work they will work without extra compensation. In all things, look for the opportunity to keep people into what they are working on.

- Explain the higher purpose behind each task.
- Link tasks to people's personal drivers.
- Build a culture of great encouragement and gratitude.
- Identify the meaning of success.

## Get active

A community that develops a bias for action will achieve amazing things. It's about moving from meeting for meeting's sake and instead meeting to advance projects.

- Create bias for action.
- Regularly check to see who is responsible for what tasks and projects.
- Date and distribute every task.
- In every action ask: "What decision are we making here?"

## Get strategic

Strategy is about knowing where you are going as a community. It is less about the big vision and more about a certainty of direction.

- Say no.
- Communicate the big picture often.
- Know your core activities and business.
- Ensure all complex strategy can be easily communicated at all levels.

**Get aligned**

Make sure that all participants in the conversation are participating for the same or at least complementary reasons. This frees up energy and decreases the friction that typically occurs when many people work together.

- ◀ Build a culture.
- ◀ Map drivers and discuss values.
- ◀ Define what a great outcome might be.
- ◀ Manage the whole person in every transaction.

It is about working smarter, not harder. One person's 'smart' might be another person's 'dumb'. Intelligent people can be their own productivity saboteurs. No matter what kind of person you are, there is a productivity style that will work for you.

## What is your personal productivity style?

When you choose to work in your best time your personal productivity increases by a minimum of 30%.

You need to choose your strategic time based on your productivity style.

You need to choose your routine and maintenance time based on your productivity style.

When we worked with one of our doctor clients, she saved six hours a week by switching one activity to her best time. One of the public relations firms we worked with increased their productivity within six months by 100% for their CEO, and their book of business doubled!

Would you like to know your productivity style?

There are two parts to your productivity style.

## Are you a planner or a crammer?

Let's give you some definition.

Think back to the last time you had to sit a big exam? Maybe think back to college … can you recall a time you had a big exam?

Are you person A?
- ◀ Did you circle the date on your calendar?
- ◀ Did you faithfully and diligently attend your tutorials?
- ◀ The night before your big exam, did you refresh yourself by reading the notes, getting a good night's sleep, waking up in the morning and sittting the exam? And you did OK?

OR …

Are you person B?
- ◀ Did you party the night before the exam?
- ◀ Get no sleep?
- ◀ Drink Red Bull and coffee all night, put toothpicks in your eyes to keep them open, get no sleep and sit the exam and voila… you did OK?
- ◀ Did you trust yourself that you would still be OK with cramming it all in?

Write it here … are you a planner or a crammer? _____

## Are you a planner or a crammer?

Here's the thing, planners hate crammers! They wonder how can you possibly get the same result and not put in the work. They are jealous.

Crammers don't understand planners. Why would you go to all that trouble when you can just leave it all to the last minute? They are also jealous!

If you are planner, maybe you need to **cram your plan**. That is, you might be wasting too much time planning when you could accelerate your results by cramming more in.

If you are a crammer, maybe you need to **plan your cram**. If you know you have a big presentation on Friday morning, you can't be having a hot date on Thursday night – because what are you going to be doing? You are going to be up creating your PowerPoint slides!

If you are a planner manager you are driving your team crazy – your constant need for updates and meetings is driving your crammer team members insane.

If you are a crammer manager, you are also driving your planner team crazy because their need for more information and details is missing from their everyday interactions with you.

# Are you a planner or a crammer?

## Here are the characteristics of a planner: Planners are systematic

- Mental preparation.
- Constant planning.
- Not last minute.
- Unconscious systems.
- Like routine.
- Tangible preparation.
- Like visuals.
- Conscious systemization.
- Think in tactical to-do sequence.
- Value time accuracy.
- Want updates.
- Judge other peoples' styles.
- Meticulously plan vacations (sometimes a year in advance) and start organizing early.
- Schedule payments in advance.
- Schedule appointments in advance.
- Don't overcommit themselves and know their commitments.
- When networking they join, book the events in their calendar and attend whenever possible.

## Here are the characteristics of a crammer: Crammers purposely procrastinate and are last-minute type people.

- RSVP late (or by the due date if it is an important occasion) and sometimes wait for a better offer.
- Spontaneous.
- Plan to attend multiple events, or they are last-minute attendees.
- Purposely procrastinate.
- Pay on due date (not often before) and sometimes late.
- Overcommit themselves.
- Join many things but don't necessarily attend them.
- Vacation plans are more last-minute, or they look for a space in their calendar and go online for last-minute deals.
- Don't schedule appointments significantly in advance; prefer to wait to see availability and preferences.
- When networking they join some memberships, don't register until the last minute and sometimes RSVP but don't attend.

As you are reading this are you wondering, "Hmm I don't think I fit either of these styles." If that's the case, maybe you are a slammer? You could be slammed in the middle of both styles!

## Slammers are a combination of both styles (planners and crammers).

It could be that you are a crammer, but the planner's way is so appealing to you—they look like they always have it together, and you desperately want to be a planner when you grow up. Or maybe you are a planner but your life is so crazy busy that you are cramming everything in, so you feel slammed in the middle of both styles.

Once you know Part A of your productivity style (e.g., planner, crammer or slammer) you can leverage your scheduling for all activities if you are able to choose the best time for you.

Write your style here: _____

Would you like to know Part B of your productivity style?

### Are you a morning bird or a night owl?

Morning birds are most productive between the hours of 7am–1pm. You wake up in the morning, your feet touch the floor and you are on! You don't even need coffee; you might like it but you don't need it. However, if at 2:30 in the afternoon, you are searching for coffee or chocolate or something that will get you through to 5pm, you are definitely a morning bird.

If you live with a night owl, don't even talk to them until they have had their morning coffee (not a glamorous or coherent conversation). They are most productive between the hours of 2pm–8pm.

Morning birds sing to let their neighbors know they are alive and survived the night and to protect their territory. They also sing to attract a mate.

In Australia we have a bird called a magpie. It is one of Australia's most highly regarded songbirds; their pitch can vary up to four octaves and they can mimic over 35 species. They have even been known to mimic humans when they live in close proximity to them.

A group of magpies will sing a short repetitive version of caroling just before dawn (dawn song), and at twilight after sundown (dusk song), in winter and spring.

Woodpeckers make their sounds in the morning in our neighborhood. When I am walking, I hear them digging for whatever they eat.

Here's the thing … if you are a morning bird:
- ◀ You need to do strategic activity first thing in the morning.
- ◀ Your brain is most engaged earlier in the day.
- ◀ You can leave the maintenance-type work for the afternoon when you don't require so much brain engagement.
- ◀ Do your business development early in the day – you are a great breakfast date, a good lunch date, but for 5pm drinks you aren't at your best. And dinner – forget about it!

If you are a night owl:
- ◀ You are most productive for strategic activity in the afternoon, so leave routine and maintenance tasks for the morning times.
- ◀ Do your business development later in the day – don't accept breakfast invitations unless critically important to the success of your business. You are a great lunch date, and fabulous for 5pm drinks. And dinner - you are on fire!

Now whom do you share your life with? I am a morning bird and share my life with night owl – there are just some things you both need to be awake for!

I prefer to minimize night presentations for clients because I am most energized in the morning. For me to be high energy at night I need to have a little "nanna nap" in the afternoon to stay energized. You know what I mean by a "nanna nap" – 10 to 20 minutes of power napping to make you feel better, just like my nanna used to do.

### Hummingbirds

Hummingbirds are most productive between 10:30am – 3pm. They have the ability to flit between time zones just like they flit between flowers looking for the next flower nectar source.

## When is the team awake?

The sweet spot of both styles is 11:30am–1pm. Big drawback – it's lunchtime! This is the time when both styles are most engaged and both awake.  Host your team meetings during this time.

Consider our body's circadian rhythm in relation to productivity styles … *circa* Latin meaning around, *diem* or *dies* – meaning day.  How can you make your productivity more meaningful every day?

We have natural cycles that our body goes through each day. These rhythms can be affected by things like sleep, shift work, light, foods we eat and exercise.  To determine your most productive timeframe, choose if you are a morning bird, a night owl … or maybe a hummingbird, and structure your most important activities in your most productive part of your day.

# action plan

Where do you need to focus your personal productivity? _____

_____

_____

_____

Which areas of the productivity matrix are your areas of enhancement? _____

_____

_____

What is your productivity style? _____

When is your best time of day? _____

What time of day do you need to focus on strategy? _____

What time of day can you focus on maintenance activities? _____

What activities can you switch to your best time? _____

_____

What is the preferred time of the people you share your life with? _____

- Focus on personal integrity.

- Keep your word.

- Make it public – get an accountability partner.

- Share your results weekly.

- Go public on social media.

- Conquer the world in 15-minute increments.

- Practice creative procrastination.

- Remember 'no' is a complete sentence.

- Productivity is about deletion … not addition.

- Make time in time.

- Plan tomorrow today.

- Increase meetings accountability and engagement.

# "Accountability breeds response-ability."

- Stephen Covey

Accountable is defined by the following words:

- ◀ Liable to being called to account
- ◀ Answerable

Similar words include: responsible, amenable and explicable. It was Henry Kissinger who said, "People think responsibility is hard to bear. It's not. I think that sometimes it is the absence of responsibility that is harder to bear. You have a great feeling of impotence."

## Focus on Personal Integrity

The late Stephen Covey shared in his book, *First Things First,* that we all have personal integrity accounts. These accounts reflect the amount of trust we have in ourselves. When we make and keep commitments, such as setting and achieving goals, we make deposits. We increase our confidence in our own trustworthiness, in our ability to make and keep commitments to ourselves and to others. A high balance in this account is a great source of strength and security, but when we don't achieve our goals, we make withdrawals, and this becomes a great source of pain.

Accountability is the foundation of Folding Time. We need to be accountable with how we invest our time, how we focus our attention and how we manage our energy. Accountability is about your personal integrity and the activities you choose to invest in.

When reflecting on my journey as a kid, teenager, entering the work place and now as a thought leader in the area of productivity – accountability is one of the most common recurring themes in my life.

Accountability can mean different things to different people. We admire those who are able to be accountable to themselves; they set a goal, keep themselves on task and then get it done. Accountability means making it public. Yes, that's right – sharing a goal with someone who can help you stay on track. Now obviously the hard work is all yours, but that level of making it public is something that drives you.

## Keep your word.

People get frustrated when others say they will do something and then don't complete it – it is the easiest way to tick someone off – when you don't do what you say you will do! So increase accountability by completing the activities and task you declare to others.

## Make it public

There are several ways you can make it public.
- ◀ You could share it with someone you trust one on one in a conversation and ask them to assist you with it.
- ◀ You could hire a coach or a mentor to help you achieve it and ask them to regularly check on you.
- ◀ You could meet regularly with someone to report on your progress.
- ◀ You could share it online through social media and allow your friends and followers to ask you about it.
- ◀ You could be part of a mastermind group that challenges you to achieve your goal.
- ◀ You could blog about your progress and share it online with those who are interested in your progress.

I have done all of these things; some work better than others.

**Tip**: Join or start a mastermind group to accelerate accountability and productivity!

## Share your results weekly

We encourage all of our clients to send their boss five (5) bullet points every week sharing their results and successes for the week. Consider this your internal public relations (PR) campaign. Keep yourself accountable and share it with those you report to so they can also share it with their leadership. This weekly review of your activities will also keep you motivated and the team around you successful.

## Get Accountability Partners

Thunderstorms generate enormous amounts of energy. Did you know the average thunderstorm releases around 10 million kilowatt-hours of energy, which is roughly equivalent to a 20-kiloton nuclear warhead? (Source: Encyclopedia Britannica.)

While tornadoes usually originate from storms, there are other events that can bring about a tornado. Sometimes tornadoes can be formed without a thunderstorm present. Whenever air – or a fluid – achieves a high enough level of rotation around a downward force, there's a chance of a vortex being created. A tornado is a violently rotating column of air in contact with the earth's surface.

Having an accountability partner is just like a tornado – the energy of combining the forces of two great minds creates momentum and accelerates results.

Two essential ways accountability helps is in declaring your goals and objectives to people who you respect and admire and never want to let down.

Each week there are two ways I have embraced accountability in my life.

Every Monday I meet with a dear friend Gina by Skype or phone. She lives in Colorado, so we connect each week to share what we have achieved during the week, the challenges we faced and what we are committing to for the upcoming week. This one-hour call is a highlight in my week. Her upbeat and crazy sense of humor and her technical and geeky approach to everything is so good to keep stretching me to do better, be better. Knowing I have to share with her also drives my behavior. We have been doing this for several years now and we often joke, "I wonder what normal people are doing while we conquer the world in our superwoman capes?" Having someone you trust and enjoy connecting with will help drive your accountability.

Every Friday my week is complete when I send an accountability email to women in my life whom I love, respect and adore. These women are on a similar journey to me with their thought leadership practices, and they are incredibly accomplished. All of them own their own practice, speak regularly around the world and are published. Two are mothers, and two of us adopt our neighbors and nephews and nieces to brag about when we are together. We aren't all located in the same area, so when we get together by phone, Skype or the luxury of face-to-face it is really awesome.

We have an agreement that every Friday (without fail) we send an accountability email to each other sharing the achievements of the week, things that frustrate us and things we are thinking about or struggling with. This email used to be all about business until one of us had a health scare, and now it is essential that each of us also report what we are doing to relax, and to take care of our relationships and ourselves.

It is easy as busy women to focus only on the financials, but we have made a pact to focus on the other areas of our lives, too. This one email definitely drives my behaviors each week. I don't want to be the only one with nothing to report, and knowing I have to share activities and projects with them makes me work even harder (especially at times when I want to slack off).

These women have been vital to the success of my practice as I also brainstorm with them, cry to them when things don't work, celebrate with them when things go well and support them when they need me. It is like a group brain – we are always looking out for each other, sharing ideas to help each other and encouraging each other. We all need that.

This is true accountability – not just a feel good club where everyone says, "There, there, it will all be OK." These women have been known to kick my b**t and use words like "get over yourself" or "get it done, stop talking about it." We all need these types of people in our lives.

If you don't have someone who comes to mind that you can be accountable to, consider hiring someone to make it happen.

For many years I tried to get healthy and lose weight. As a yo-yo dieter in the worst way, I tried many techniques, including a personal trainer. It wasn't until finding my latest personal trainer that a mind shift finally happened.

Sometimes the right person comes into your life and they have a big impact on you. I had hired other personal trainers over the years; however, it seems this one was the right fit for me.

Why get a personal trainer when I could do all the same exercises at home in my home gym? Let me paint a picture for you of our home gym: it is complete with state of the art treadmill, free weights, benches, heavy bag for boxing (in pink of course) with matching pink boxing gloves, a full sound system and a TV. And yet I prefer to go to the studio to work out. Why? Because the trainer keeps me accountable; he makes me work harder than I thought possible. There are times I doubt I can do what he says and yet he encourages me to go further, try harder and dig deeper.

When working with women in our Mentoring Program, an easy way to assist them with staying accountable to their goals is by checking in by phone or text. Some of the women in the program text weekly their goals and achievements, others schedule a phone call. We can also use technology to help us stay accountable.

## Go Public on Social media

A friend embarked on creating a healthier version of herself through exercise and diet. She generously shared some of her journey with her Facebook friends by regularly posting blogs, updates and photos of her progress. This high level of public accountability also helped her stay focused because she had a worldwide cheer squad encouraging and supporting her to her goals. We have watched her lose weight, make fun of her personal trainer (in the kindest way) and participate in distance running. All of her friends will tell you how proud they are of her, and we regularly see comments about her "inspirational" journey posted by others.

David Siteman Garland, host of *The Rise to the Top,* is passionate about helping experts dominate with their brands online. When he embarked on his fitness journey he booked a photo shoot and declared it to the online world so he also was able to leverage a community online.

Don't underestimate the power of your global community for accountability.

If you want to increase accountability in your life personally or professionally, find an accountability partner and declare a goal that you can check your progress at 30, 60 and 90 days.

## Conquer the World in 15 minutes

No one has an hour anymore; however, people will invest 15 minutes with you.

## 15 minutes is the true secret of productivity.

It is a powerful amount of time that people will give you and that you can invest in projects, meetings and taking actions.

**Set the clock** – Play a game with time and see how much you can achieve in 15 minutes.

Dr. Alan Zimmerman said. "There is never enough time … unless you're serving it" – we say choose to invest 15 minutes of time! Make time serve you.

In 15 minutes you can:

- ◀ Tackle your inbox and clear email.
- ◀ Meditate.
- ◀ Exercise or go for a walk.
- ◀ Conduct a real conversation.
- ◀ Make a healthy meal.
- ◀ Make a prospecting call.
- ◀ Send two handwritten notes.
- ◀ Back up your computer.
- ◀ Do your weekly paper filing.
- ◀ Pay your bills online.
- ◀ Fold laundry.

The list is endless. When you play the 15-minute game you can set an alarm and do something for 15 minutes – you will be surprised how much you achieve in this time.

**Social media management** – If you want to stay hyper-productive with your time online, consider investing only 15 minutes in the morning to update your status, review blogs and connect. Invest 15 minutes in the afternoon to respond and review.

**Write a book in just 15 minutes a day** – In 2007, one of the participants in our Mentoring Program had been complaining that she wanted to write a book but didn't have time. We had heard her say this many times, so we finally said to her in a very exasperated tone, "Just write the damn book! If you write for 15 minutes every day you will be done by the end of the year." Of course she didn't believe us, but she diligently wrote for 15 minutes every day. On the days she didn't write she had to make up the time the next day. We started in January. On December 18th, she opened her first box of books with her name proudly on the cover. We were beyond proud of her and know her book will impact her industry.

**Choose time abundance** – When speaking of time we need to choose abundance rather than scarcity. Instead of saying, "I don't have time" replace this with, "I didn't choose to spend time on that." Try it out! It is very liberating.

**Change the way you talk about time** – instead of saying, "I'll work out if I have time," say, "I'm going to work out this morning before I go to work" – don't leave activities to chance; make a conscious decision to talk about time positively with an action plan.

**Practice Creative Procrastination - Waste time - don't kill time**.
Wasting time is good if you are seeking a creative solution and thinking through options, choices, strategies, ideas and concepts.

Chris Anderson explores this idea in his book *Free,* where he shares that waste in nature is good. We often hear that wasting time is bad but as Anderson points out, nature wastes life in search of a better life.

Consider the example of a dandelion flower. As little children we seek pleasure picking these flowers and blowing the flower top, watching the seeds scatter across the field and in the air. This is a fabulous opportunity to watch every seed become a new opportunity for reproduction of the dandelion plant. This is a great example where waste is good.

Wasting time can be powerful if it helps to grow a new idea, reenergizes you or helps you recover after a busy schedule. Let's not kill time; let's focus on how to creatively waste time.

## Practice Procrastination – Wait ... now hurry up!

During a Disney trip, it was fascinating watching the lines waiting for rides. People would rush to get in a line and then wait ... and wait! You could hurry up your wait by getting a quick pass that told you when to return for the ride (especially the more popular ones) and then ... you could wait some more! Hurry up ... and wait.

**Take a brief pause** – A moment to stop and reflect: to pause what you are doing, to think before you speak ... these strategies can help you make a smarter move.

In his book *Getting Things Done,* David Allen shares that smart people procrastinate! I love this, and this doesn't give you an excuse to not get things done. It means that taking time to pause is powerful.

Brian Tracy in his book *Eat that Frog* shares that time management is really life management. We need to know the true sense of urgency for some things, and then we need to realize that in life we need to practice procrastination.

Here are ways you can practice procrastination:

- ◀ Keep a list.
- ◀ Sequence your list.
- ◀ Put pressure on yourself.
- ◀ Think like you only have one day to complete something.
- ◀ Take one full day off every week (or start monthly if you can't do this weekly) to just do nothing.
- ◀ Be your own cheerleader and stop following the requests of others.
- ◀ Create silent zones where you won't allow technology of any kind to permeate the space.

**Get a procrastination pal** – No, not someone you can procrastinate with!  Identify someone you can call when you are procrastinating who will help you get on track. Let them know they are your designated procrastination pal and when you call them they have permission to help you get focused and moving (and that includes telling you to get off you b**t and do something!).

**Know the contribution you make** – Procrastination is a great tool to determine where is the best place for you to contribute and make an impact. It forces you to step back and review.

## Productivity is about deletion ... not addition

The old style productivity or time management programs will teach you how to arrange all the activities you have in systems including calendars, task lists, folders … and while this is all good information, it is flawed!

Productivity is not about addition; it's about deletion!

It's not about adding more to your already full plate, it's about deleting activities from your plate.

One of the most effective ways to delete or delegate activities from your already growing list of responsibilities is to say no … and say it often.

We need to say NO often … and over and over again.  Clients from around the world struggle with this powerful word. People want to be seen as team players and feel that if they say no they might offend someone.

## No is a full sentence.

No doesn't require explanation.

No means no.

I love no. I think it is a great word to become your friend if you want to sound more productive.

Of course the power of no is all in your delivery (tone, inflection and facial expressions).

A few ways to help you say no more easily include:

**Understand your priorities and have them in writing** – This could include having your calendar kept up to date with activities and your goals posted in clear view to remind you.

If someone invites you to an event, you can refer to your calendar and comment, "Thank you for thinking of me; however, I am already committed at that time."

Before you say no also **understand the full extent** of what you are being asked to do or attend. Sometimes we think there is more (or maybe even less) involved than is true. Ask several questions before giving your response.

◀ Am I the best person to do this?
◀ Does this timing work for me?
◀ Do I have all the information required to make this decision?

You could also ask yourself another simple question; **"Is this the best use of my time right now**?" This simple but effective question will allow you to discontinue working on something and refocus on what matters.

**Deletion might mean delegation** – You might also like to ask yourself, "Am I the best person to be working on this?" Are you investing time in activities that could potentially be delegated or outsourced to others that could help you achieve your goals?

In his book *18 minutes*, Peter Bregman suggests, "We need to quickly and confidently identify and reduce our extraneous commitments, to know for sure whether we should deal with something or avoid it and to manage our own desire to be available always." His advice is powerful when considering collaborating with others, trying to turn down an invitation and in our everyday responses during emails and meetings.

**Keep your answers short** when responding with a no – if you attempt to over-explain or give too much detail, you might sound like you are making an excuse. No one wants to hear that.

If you do need to say no to a task or project, can you **recommend someone else** so that you are also able to assist the person making the request?

We all know we don't have time to do everything; we only have time to do what matters.

To allow you to achieve what matters, consider these strategies to help incorporate no into your language:

**Just say, "No"** - No doesn't require an explanation. You can still gracefully decline an invitation for a social event or a meeting request on the condition that you do it with kindness and don't go into a long-winded explanation.  If you can't attend an event simply say, "Thank you for kindly thinking of me." That's it – nothing else required.

Deletion is a choice (just like addition): however, some of the most productive people I know do less … not more! What can you choose to delete today?

Have you ever found yourself at a social gathering, holding onto your glass of wine as you survey the room, and asking yourself, "Why did I ever say yes to this party?" Me too!

Because of this, decide that unless you are absolutely certain you are available and absolutely want to attend an event, consider your first response to be "no." If you are going to respond to a kind invitation with a no, be sensitive in how you deliver this and also don't over-explain why you aren't attending.

A simple, "Thank you for your kind invitation, however I am unable to join you," is all the host wants to hear. Don't be that person who waits until the last minute to respond because you are waiting for a better offer or feel bad saying no – just say no!

Some friends will tell you I have been known to say no first and they respond with, "Before you say no … just let me tell you more about it." It makes me giggle knowing that they understand me, and we can joke about it. Don't get me wrong, I love a party more than the next person and want to make sure that the time I'm not working, I'm investing with people and activities that make the most of every minute.

I heard a great quote once (and wish I knew the source): "I don't want to be sitting on my front porch ever repeating the same story." I love that! It inspires me to say no so I can say a big YES to more.

In the book *Anything You Want,* Derek Sivers says, "When you say no to most things you leave room in your life to throw yourself completely into that rare thing that makes you say, 'hell yeah.'" I love this quote.

While writing this book I declined many fun opportunities (writing in the summer while friends were heading to the beach). It is often hard to say no to people we care about, clients we really enjoy working with and goals we want to achieve. The reason to say no is to stay clear and focused on your goal of completing a project.

Saying no allows you to say yes to activities that energize you.

What do you need to say no to so you can say, "**Hell yeah!**"?

## Make time in time.
## Cleverly use aspects of time
## to increase capacity.

In the *Harry Potter* books, Hermione carried a time-turner. This was an hourglass on a necklace that allowed her to travel through time and be in two places at once. Each turn of the hourglass equaled one hour of time. It was essential in using this time-turner that she never be seen by her past or future version of herself, unless of course she was aware she was using the time-turner. This allowed her to attend multiple classes at the same time and accelerate her schooling. Oh, some days how we wish we had Hermione's time-turner!

Without a time-turner we need to make time in time. We can cleverly use aspects of time to increase capacity.

Making time in time is about combining activities, e.g., reading journals while waiting at your doctor's office for your appointment, or hosting a walk and talk meeting while you walk from one office building to the next. While employed by Australia's largest bank, my manager was an amazingly successful woman who was the queen of making time in time. Her busy calendar required walking between big corporate offices regularly and there was a tunnel between the head office and our office. Often we would have walk and talks to accelerate project process, share learnings from internal clients and agree on action steps for marketing initiatives. Sometimes we felt like Teenage Mutant Ninja Turtles as we scurried back and forth - we did accomplish an enormous amount of work during those times!

One of my mentors might recall I attended a haircut with him because it was the only time he had available that day, and he wasn't going to be doing anything but sitting in a chair patiently allowing his hairdresser to work his magic. We scoped out a project plan for a conference during one haircut – never underestimate the power of making time in time. OK, so maybe you don't want to follow someone to a haircut (funny); however, there will be many times you could leverage the time of people around you.

**Use elevators** to make time in time. During your elevator ride you can silence your cell and do a 30 second check on your appearance: pop in a breath mint, straighten your outfit, check your hair and make-up, apply lipstick and adjust jewelry.

**Six-minute theory** – If you invest 10% of every hour you will maximize the remaining 90% of that hour – do this for one day and watch your productivity skyrocket. You can make time in time by using just small increments of time to accelerate results.

## Plan tomorrow today

Investing less than 1% of your time today will make you 10 times more effective.

Have you ever written something on a to-do list, just so you can cross it off?

Why do we do this? We want and need some sense of satisfaction that we actually got something done today. By investing 10 minutes at the end of the day you can take a moment to make a note of your successes from today – voilà – fixes the need to write and cross off!

If you want to ensure that when you leave the office you feel more in control and stop thinking about all the little details of the day, investing 10 minutes at the end of the day will help you.

**Start tomorrow's to-do list** – Taking a few moments to create new list for tomorrow will save you thinking about them tonight. It will help you realize what's important to approach first in the day.

**Check commitments** – Scan your calendar to see where your first appointment is and if you need to do any preparation for it. Find out where it is located and calculate how much time you need to get there.

**Clean-up** – Take a moment to wash out your coffee mug, throw away the trash, file your papers and check your outbox (to make sure all emails were sent). A few minutes of clean-up makes you look and feel more organized.

**Carry reading** – If you want to stay on top of reading of physical journals, articles and magazines, start a reading file and carry it with you overnight. If you have spare moments you can enjoy catching up.

**Know whom you can connect** – Often driving from home in Doylestown to meet clients in King of Prussia (weird name for a suburb right?) can take between 40–60 minutes depending on traffic. We always know who to call on the drive (hands free of course) because it is a great way to use drive time productively.

**Shut down** – Turn off every piece of technology you can and shut down systems to signify to yourself it is also time to shut down your brain from the projects you have been working on.

## Meetings - Accountability and Engagement
### Agendas always
Be prepared (just like a boy scout) for every conversation and every situation.

Have you ever tried to listen to the radio station and it wasn't quite tuned in correctly – the static noise is so distracting! To ensure your communications are more productive and clear consider having an agenda.

Robert Stephenson Smyth Baden-Powell established the Boy Scouts Association in Britain in 1910. When it was set up in USA it became Boy Scouts of America, one of the largest youth organizations in the country; the motto was, "Be prepared." Agendas are a vital component of a meeting. We all know an agenda in a meeting helps create a more productive meeting; however, have you considered having agendas in other areas of your life?

**When you answer the phone** you could say, "G'Day, what's on your agenda for our phone call today?" This allows your caller to quickly get to the point and no time is wasted in small talk. We find this technique has helped hundreds of clients increase the effectiveness of their phone time

**When you meet with someone important to you** - Next time you **meet with your mentor,** ensure you have an agenda prepared to maximize your time. When I was being mentored early in my speaking career, I always had an agenda so if I was fortunate to have even five minutes of my mentor's time I had a question for him to help me with. It made all those small amounts of time very valuable.

**Understand other people's agendas** – Sometimes communication fails because we are focused only on our agenda and oblivious to the other agendas in the conversation. A simple question I like to ask people when I meet is, "Are there any other agendas I need to be aware of?" This will help raise any hidden or undisclosed agendas to accelerate the conversation.

## How to Set Agendas

Often when working with sales teams on a new client pitch or product launch, they ask if there is a secret to a successful pitch or meeting. Yes - set an agenda.

Too often we run into the presentation with our 'spiel' and don't take time to stop and find out what others in the meeting want to know or hear.

Listed below are strategies you can apply to ensure your sales pitch, or any meetings you have, are more effective.

## Before the meeting

**Phone ahead** – Contact your potential new client and confirm the meeting time, location, power options (i.e., power points) and the number of people attending. This allows you to have sufficient copies of material if required.

**Find out who the decision makers are** – As part of your confirmation call, find out the names and titles of all people attending. This will assist you in preparing and may give an indication of who the decision maker is.

## During the Meeting

**Write up an agenda** – Before you open your laptop or launch into your presentation, take a few minutes to write up an agenda that everyone can see.

**Use a Whiteboard, iPad or blank paper to capture agenda items** – Ask everyone, "What is on your agenda for our meeting today?" Some people may be surprised you asked the question, so take time to allow people to think about their response.

**Use different color pens for each person's agenda item** – If you have a white board or flipchart, use different colors for each person. If you are using a piece of paper, use colors if you have them. This allows you to quickly identify what is important to each person.

**Check the timing of the meeting** – Confirm with the attendees, "Do we have until 1pm together today?" This will allow all participants to agree or provide you with information if they have to leave earlier to attend to another matter. This can be critical when pitching a new product or idea, as you want to ensure that the decision makers are available for the important components of your discussion.

**Identify global (strategic) and local (specific) agenda items** – When reviewing the agenda, look for distinction between the two types of agenda items and make note of who they belong to. This will help you address them throughout the meeting.

**Ask how everyone feels about the meeting** – It is important to get a sense for how people are feeling. This can include the investment in time they are making, anticipation of what you have to offer, or concerns about the product or company. In business we don't always take time to acknowledge feelings that enter a meeting; however, feelings affect decision-making.

**Keep asking for agenda items** – You may need to continue asking, "Is there anything else?" If everyone says no, you may need to ask again, "If there was something else, what would it be?" This allows everyone time to declare every agenda item on their mind.

**Check for hidden agendas** – In most meetings there is also a hidden agenda. It is simple to find out what this is – just ask the question, "What other agendas are there for this meeting?" Alternatively you might state, "There always seems to be another agenda with most meetings I attend, is there another agenda today?" It is important to find out if there are other drivers, decision-making criteria or other concerns before you begin the meeting.

This may seem like a long process but it so valuable.

Setting agendas for a meeting shows potential (or existing) clients that you value their time, want to cover information or content that is relevant to them, and you haven't come in to just 'sell' your services or product.

When you invest in setting an agenda you can speed up the meeting by addressing each item, focus your presentation on the aspects most important to your potential client, and demonstrate respect for their investment in time and their concerns or feelings about the meeting.

If you hold regular team meetings it is also valuable to have a specific agenda and allow an opportunity at the beginning of the meeting to add additional items, assess people's feelings and uncover hidden agendas for that meeting.

## Meeting Effectiveness

When I was a little girl I was fascinated with the Jack-in-the-box toy! I would squeal with delight when the clown popped out (as if it was the first time I had seen it). The quick surprise and fast action always caused a response in me.

If you want to accelerate your meetings, be like the Jack-in-the-box – stand up!

A standing meeting is a quick meeting!

While running large teams in corporate Australia, we held standing meetings. These meetings can be five to fifteen minutes in length and because you are standing, people are more likely to get to the point more quickly and want to keep the conversation progressing.

If you want to handle the constant interruptions of people visiting your cube or office during the day, when they walk into your space … stand up! They won't know if you are coming or going (which can be funny to watch their faces)!

One of the executives I worked with in the cable industry feels this one technique has saved him hours weekly. As a very senior leader he was constantly sharing his wisdom with team members when they entered his office, and now he applies this technique. He shared recently that people get to the point more quickly and many now don't interrupt, they schedule time with him instead of random daily interruptions – very cool!

# Host a Tele-coffee

Best meeting ever!

This is where you make a coffee, and I make a coffee, and we talk on the telephone – takes no more than 15 minutes!

You can build relationships with virtual coffees. Think of all the time you are saving No travel, no fabulous outfit required, no overpriced Starbucks coffee price – just you, your attendee and an agenda.

If you want to conduct this virtual meeting consider a few guidelines:

**Have an agenda** – Just like a live meeting, this quick and effective meeting requires a purpose to meet an agenda. Send the agenda in the meeting request to ensure all parties are prepared.

**Keep it to 15 minutes** – Most people can engage in conversations for short periods of time and you will be astounded how much you can achieve in this small, but productive, time increment.

**Agree on outcomes** – Before the tele-coffee is complete, spend the last two minutes determining your action plan and agreed action items.

**Use video** – If you want to increase the engagement use video tools including Skype or Google+ Hangout. This requires you both to be involved and not multi-task i.e., check email or get distracted.

**Host tele-cocktails** – If you know someone well or it is Friday afternoon, consider a tele-cocktail – too much fun! This can be fun with girlfriends or family living overseas.

# Meeting Management
## Strategies to increase meeting effectiveness

When you are asking people to invest time, you want to ensure your highest level of integrity to ensure their time and attention is maximized. To enable meetings to be more effective try these strategies:

**Group client meetings on the same day** – If you are involved in business development or client follow up, structure your week so that you can group client related calls in the same day. This can be an efficient use of time and allows you to stay focused. One of the strategies shared by thought leader Stacey Hanke is that she sets a time block in her calendar and doesn't move from her desk until all calls are made. If you can chain yourself to your desk and diligently get through those calls, you create momentum and momentum creates results.

**Design meetings** to be 20 minutes or 40 minutes (never 30 or 60) – most people fill whatever time is allocated for the meeting. If you want to look like a hero shorten your meetings immediately. One of my clients in the cable industry did an experiment and over the course of a week she reduced every meeting she was in control of – her team loved her! They were so appreciative that she gave them time back; they found they were more productive, more energized to attend any future meetings with her, and they have done the same thing with their team members. Once again, momentum creates results. Can you shorten your regular meetings? I promise you will still achieve as much (if not more), however you will find the meeting has a greater sense of urgency to get more done quickly and move along.

## Host Effective Teleconferences

Have you ever been on one of those calls where you hear all the beeps, background noise, someone's dog barking and the host says stupidly obvious statements like:

"Did someone just join?" "Who just joined?"

Teleconferences can be highly productive if the host is focused and the team is willing to give their undivided attention to the meeting (as if they were meeting in real life). Minimum time plus high energy results in productive teleconferences.

Many of you know (and I have been guilty of this) using our EMV (email voice, this term was discovered in the book *Crazy Busy* by Dr. Edward Hallowell) while attending teleconference; we check our email, multi-task and totally disrespect the people on the call.

My husband works with a technology company and every Monday they have an enormous amount of conference calls. I have listened over the years to some of the worst examples of teleconference behaviors, and I wonder if you can relate to some of the things I have witnessed below:
- ◄ Really long calls.
- ◄ Too many people on the line.
- ◄ People using cell phones with bad reception.
- ◄ Asking the question "Who just joined?"
- ◄ Being put on mute and not paying attention.
- ◄ Someone's dog barking in the background.
- ◄ Side bar conversations.
- ◄ Side tracked conversations.
- ◄ No agenda.

To avoid these bad practices consider the following strategies:

**Set agenda and guidelines**– Regardless of how long the call will be, set a specific agenda and circulate to all participants in advance. Allocate specific timeframes to each speaker. If they have an allocated agenda item, every participant should adhere to that time frame. Also ensure the team knows the rules of your teleconferences to increase effectiveness.

**Understand functionality** - Know how to use all aspects of the technology and write instructions for others you can leave it beside the phone or in your boardroom. Be effective at muting bells and sounds, know how to record and minimize noise levels.

**Turn off cells** - That's right, turn to silent or turn it off - nobody is indispensable! In teleconferences it is rude to answer calls or send text messages while another meeting is occurring. You have voicemail, and your callers will always be able to reach you. One of my media clients has a basket outside the meeting room and everyone is required to drop in their cell phone before entering the room – their meetings are more productive and people are focused.

**Keep quiet** – It is difficult to hear on a teleconference if people are shuffling papers, sending text messages, heavy breathing, having side bar conversations – don't do it. If you are on a large call use the relevant keys to mute your phone. Be still and listen to the whole conversations.

**Short conversations** - Not everyone around you wants to hear your plans or unnecessary details, so keep conversations short and on point. Remember, the cost of teleconference calls is expensive (think of adding up everyone's salary on the call … what does that meeting cost)?

**One speaker** - This courtesy assists participants in hearing the entire conversation. On some teleconference facilities if one person speaks it cuts out the sound for everyone else.

**Time sensitive** – Where possible, restrict calls to business hours (unless the job indicates otherwise). Cell phones and teleconferences have made us more accessible to other team members; be sensitive to different time zones and people's personal lives.

**Conduct on landline** - If you are on your cell, you may experience dropouts or low signal areas making the call frustrating (for you and other attendees), and you may miss out on important information. Calls to cells can be expensive so try to save money with landlines if possible.

**Be considerate** – Keep conversations on topic, don't move from the agreed agenda unless vital, keep information relevant to participants and don't use language or jargon that may not be understood by everyone (especially when dealing with technology or complicated projects).

**Create actions** – At the end of each call, confirm the action plan, agreed owners for each action item and restate objectives. Never have a call just for the sake of a call– every request of someone's time needs to be considered to ensure time is maximized.

**Halve the time** – Can you take half as long to achieve twice as much? Try it. Experiment with timing to shorten the call and increase engagement.

Teleconferences are a vital part of business. To achieve greater results from this productive meeting style, apply these strategies and your teleconferences will achieve your objective.

## Spotlight: Accountability Creates Momentum with Megan Kristel

When I first met Megan, she was eight months pregnant and wearing a stunning black dress and high black patent stilettos! She caught my attention because she not only looked fabulous, but she was probably one of the most glamorous pregnant women I had ever seen. At this networking event, we discovered she had just left her corporate high-pressure job where she had excelled at every level and she had created an image and style company – brand new, while eight months pregnant!

I liked her immediately. There were many things I admired: her tenacity, her sense of humor and her drive. Something that really stood out about her was the commitment to this new business – that she would do whatever it took to make it a success. As we spoke more, she got involved in my mentoring program for women. She was one of the most successful case studies ever in our program. Her diligence, her commitment to building systems that were scalable in her business and her absolute love for her clients contributed to the success she is today.

She took copious notes, did all her homework, recreated systems, customized templates and followed every piece of advice. She was, and still is, brilliant.

Megan Kristel, founder and CEO of Kristel Closets is the perfect illustration of someone who demonstrates accountability in all aspects of her personal and professional life. As one of the most successful thought leaders in the area of personal image and style, she has grown her practice from a one-person operation out of her home to a diverse team that works with leading companies across the USA.  Having created such a successful practice, Megan also mentors other stylists create their own business and is the force behind Style Maker University.

One of the secrets of her success is a strong drive and high level of accountability. Megan is not only accountable to herself, but she recruits her family and trusted friends to ensure she stays focused on the best use of her time.

Everyone needs someone to "**hold their feet to the fire,**" declares Megan Kristel.

Personally, she works with a trainer to keep her fitness and stamina at peak levels, and professionally she seeks mentors who can hold her accountable to her aggressive goals. We had the opportunity to ask her about her accountability strategies, and she shared the following:

**Schedule each minute** – When she is her most productive self (which she will tell you is not each and every day), she schedules her day down to the minute (generally in 15 minute increments). This highly scheduled plan allows a sense of achievement all day and she can cross things off her list (even if it is only the satisfaction of making oatmeal for her gorgeous girls).

**Motivate with visual reminders** – Writing her to-do list on post-it notes; it feels great to cross it off and throw in the trash!

**Schedule date nights** – Megan schedules regular date nights with her busy and talented husband, and they also make date nights with their two girls a priority. I had heard of date nights with your partner but haven't heard parents mention this for their kids – it's a great way to grow relationships. She explained that with their busy travel schedules this was an essential time with the girls to ensure they feel heard, are coping OK, and talking about things that are important to them. I love this strategy.

**Schedule Sunday** – A non-negotiable appointment every Sunday to check the numbers of her practice, and her personal finance keeps her on track. Diligently checking expenses, line by line, confirms projections and cash flow. There is significant satisfaction of seeing numbers increase.

**Ask others** – She regularly seeks advice and input of people important to her that provide a progress report; people who will speak truth and not let her get away with things.

**Choose integrity** – Decide daily to be the best you can today, to do what you say you will do and determine what you can accomplish today – that's your choice.

One of the drivers she shared is learned from her parents; while on this planet she has a responsibility to contribute to it. For the sake of her girls, she wants to role model to them how they can grow to be influential in their worlds.

Increased accountability equals increased productivity. When you approach each day knowing you need to do what you say you will do and understand the impact that has on the planet – now that's productive!

## Spotlight: Get in the Accountability Zone with Sam Silverstein

As an infopreneur, business expert, and international author, Sam Silverstein's battle cry of "*No More Excuses*" (also the title of his book) has been heard by companies and business professionals the world over.

We interviewed Sam about the role of accountability in the industries he is part of and ways that we could bring more accountability into our everyday lives. He shared the following leadership strategies with us:

**Implement proactive accountability** – In both your personal and professional life explore opportunities to be accountable. Sam shared this is about knowing what you are accountable for: in his great blog he says, "When we relate this to managing our time, we only have so much time during the day to achieve what it is that we need to achieve. What activities are we doing that are not moving us towards the achievement of our strategic intent? Because if we can figure out what's not working for us, we can eliminate that and create space to then bring in new activities so we can grow as individuals and grow our organizations."

**Bring accountability partners into your life** – We have detailed this early in this chapter and were delighted to hear him share this as a key strategy. I like public accountability, and when you declare it I believe you do it!

**Build an accountability circle** – This strategy is similar to a mastermind concept: a group of people you can share your strategic plan with to help keep you focused and accountable to that plan.

When asked about the trends for accountability Sam believes that as companies get a leaner workforce they are looking for successful people to increase their accountability – this will become even more important. He says, "Accountability is today's competitive advantage. We need to reclaim market share and win the hearts of a hyper-discerning consumer."

Something he said really stuck with me: accountability is self-discipline. He explained that the people he knows that have achieved great success in their personal and professional lives demonstrate self-discipline, which he defined as focus, tracking results and holding themselves accountable.

## Spotlight: Exceed and Excel by Example with Fred Beans

If you live anywhere near the Philadelphia area you have heard of Fred Beans.

This amazing man started with one gas station in the late 1950's, with a loan co-signed by his mother!

From humble beginnings, he has grown the Fred Beans company brand to include Fred Beans Collision Centers, AutoExpress, NAPA of Doylestown, Autorent of Doylestown and Fred Beans Parts. He currently owns and operates 19 dealerships in the greater Philadelphia area. He will also proudly share that he employs 1650 people in the "Fred Beans family."

Recently we were privileged to partner with Fred on a project, and we interviewed him about some of the biggest challenges faced by diverse businesses like his, and he shared great insights with me. Fred is someone that demonstrates a high level of accountability – he has invested significantly in his company and his community and is a man of integrity.

**Be prepared to change** - When asked about the biggest challenges to his business he shared that business is now more Internet dependent and customers have adapted to Internet shopping. 50% of their business is a result of selling cars through incoming phone and Internet leads. He shared that some car dealers have been slow to change from conventional ways of advertising such as newspaper and radio. Radio has been diluted even more by XM radio, and similarly, television has been diluted by cable television. Fred believes that for the average consumer, given the choice between Google and his TV set, he might **give up his television for Google**.

**Hire right** – One of the secrets of the Fred Beans brand is strong engagement from their team and the families that buy from his dealerships. Fred shared they hire the right people that are enthusiastic and have motivation on the inside and something they bring to work every day. His leadership believes it is their job to help create a team and bring the best out of people through leadership. He shared it really starts with whom they hire and the skill sets they come to work with.

**Prioritize the right activities** – There are only three simple priorities for the Fred Beans brand: taking care of customers, selling cars and managing inventory. He shared that all team members need to spend more time on the floor with him. One of his heroes is Sam Walton, founder of Walmart, who had a reputation that often if someone called for him they couldn't find him in the office because he was on the floor with his customers.

**Be accountable and exceed** customer's expectations – The sale of a car and the relationship with a customer is not a spelled out process like building a car, working on a production line or assembling an automobile. It is about **interactions with customers** and there are so many disconnects – he shared accountability is a big challenge for the car industry.

Be passionate – Fred shared he believes we have to **set goals** and objectives for everybody to work toward every day **with passion and humility and a caring attitude**.

I observed many quality traits while working with Fred. So many things impressed me and here are the three characteristics I witnessed every time I worked with him:

**Duty** – Fred believes in his duty to his country, his family, his customers and his community. He is focused on always giving back and exploring how he can help more people. He shared that it was his duty to leave this world a better place. He thought if a guy like him could build a business, then he could help other guys build a business, grow their community and support their families.

**Wisdom** – Fred is an avid reader, always quoting books, sharing resources with me and buying books by the caseload to share with his team. Having been in his personal library many times, I was in awe of the depth and breadth of his book collection.

**Generosity** – Fred believes in mentors, being a mentor and seeking out mentors. His commitment to his own development is so evident; he constantly strives to learn how to do more, be better and share more. He still does regular field trips to other dealers to learn from them and their best practices. You only have to look around the town of Doylestown to also see his generosity to his community. He often said, "I can't sing and I can't dance … but I can **leave my mark** by running a business, being responsible and giving back to our community."

Thank you Fred Beans for being an example, for making an impact on thousands of lives in Bucks County (and beyond) and for being such a generous example to all generations.

**That's how accountability is related to Folding Time.** We only have 86,400 seconds in a day: that's 1440 minutes, 24 hours – we all get the same amount. We have to be accountable for how we invest that time. Once spent, we don't get the time back.  How will you be more accountable for the time you invest today?

Who is someone you admire that demonstrates exceptional accountability? Write their name here:

_____

## action plan

Make an appointment to interview them for 15 minutes by phone.
**Ask them, "How do you use accountability in your personal and professional life?"**

Write their responses here: _____

_____

_____

_____

_____

_____

Now what will you do differently as a result of reading this chapter? _____

_____

_____

_____

_____

- Walk into a room assuming everyone wants to play with you.
- Listen with your eyes.
- Live in the moment.
- Create a productive language pallette.
- Eliminate urgency.
- Replace red flag words.
- Stop 'shoulding' on people.
- Stop saying, "Can I pick your brain?"
- Talk time.
- Always ask a question.
- Make an impactful impression.
- Trap your thoughts.
- Communicate to the left and right brain.
- Demonstrate impactful integrity.
- Surround yourself with VIPs (Very Inspiring People).
- Practice engagement mastery.
- Be strategically social.
- Be someone's hero.
- Consciously celebrate.
- Demonstrate personal integrity.
- Be purposefully engaging.

# "Full engagement is the intersection of integrity and impact."

- Neen James

Engagement is how you focus your attention. In Folding Time, once you have the foundation of accountability with time you are able to determine where you can best focus your attention.

Have you ever had a conversation with someone and they were only half listening? Do you remember how you felt? Do you remember some of your frustrations? Productive people know that giving someone your undivided attention will help accelerate productivity because conversations will be powerful while both parties are fully present in the moment.

## Communication Engagement

**Walk into a room assuming everyone wants to play with you.** This has always been my assumption, even as a little girl, and has continued into adulthood. When entering a room, make an assumption that all of the people want to meet you, and you will show up with more impact. You will be poised, confident and your body language will reflect your anticipation to have great conversations with everyone you meet.

**Listen with your eyes.** When we first moved to the USA from Sydney, Australia we met an adorable five-year-old called Donovan (he is my next door neighbor). While seated in the kitchen of his home, his mum Eileen and I were chatting over a coffee and Donovan and I were in a huge debate! We were arguing about which Pokémon character I really was! He asked me a question, and I answered it. At the same time Eileen asked me a question, and I answered it.

Donovan then walked over and said, rather irritated and loudly while stomping his little feet, "Neen you are not listening to me!" I replied (also a little annoyed), "Yes, Donovan, I was listening to you, you asked me this question and this was my response."

He came over to me and grabbed my face in his two little hands, turned it towards him and said, "Neen, listen with your eyes." He was five – such wisdom.

We need to listen with our eyes more; we need to stop having half conversations, or conversations where one party is in the room and the other is screaming to try and make a point.

To listen with your eyes more consider these strategies:

**Stop multi (multi)-tasking** – Give someone your undivided attention when you are with them so you can engage in the conversation. A study published by *USA Today* quoted uSamp senior vice president, "We really have managers captured 24/7, we're all tethered." Choose to focus on someone instead of on your technology.

**Don't talk through walls** – If you are in another room don't continue a conversation; wait until you have re-entered the room so you can look people in the eye. I try this at home, however am not always successful; it is a great place to start practicing it.

**Use video** – If you have the opportunity to convert a phone call to a video call when speaking remotely, use video to increase effectiveness.

Albert Mehrabian, a professor at UCLA, is often misquoted about his communication effectiveness study when people share that 55% of communication is body language, 38% is tone and 7% is words. Some have taken these statistics and presented them as fact without realizing he was referring to communicating about feelings and attitudes and when you are in rapport with someone. It is the part about 'being in rapport' with someone that is often left out of conversations when referencing his work.

Dale Carnegie said, "Listen with your eyes and your ears." This is great advice.

Richard Carlson, author of *Don't Sweat the Small Stuff*, says, "Effective listening is more than simply avoiding the bad habit of interrupting others while they are speaking or finishing their sentences. It's being content to listen to the entire thought of someone rather than waiting impatiently for your chance to respond."

**Stop using EMV or email voice** – In Dr. Edward Hallowell's book *Crazy Busy* there is a great chapter on different words used for the way we handle our busy lives. We especially loved this term because as soon as we read it we knew what he meant. Have you ever been on the phone with someone and realized they were checking their email while talking to you? They have a distant sound – it is subtle but unmistakable!  If you want to engage in conversation, that means eliminating the distraction of your cell phone or laptop and STOP checking your email while chatting to people. It's disrespectful and such a lost opportunity to communicate and make others feel valued.

How can you listen with your eyes more today?

**Live in the moment –** Life gets busy; we get distracted. We are often focused on what we want instead of where we are.  I was reading Kevin Hall's book *Aspire* (one of my all-time favorite books) –he was mentored by Stephen Covey and shared his personal motto was to "Live life in crescendo." Wow, what a great way to be constantly looking forward. He goes on to say that he is all about focusing on contribution, not achievement.

In our lives we can focus on being present, being connected, being engaged to ensure that everyone we meet, have a conversation with or are in the presence of, feels like they are the most important person we are spending time with in that moment.

In Kevin's book he has a secret word: Genshai. This means we should never treat another person in a manner that would make them feel small. Sometimes in our eagerness to get things done we forget to live in the moment and be fully present.

Who do you need to live in the moment with today?

# We are networking, not connecting

In the fabulous book *Fascinate* by Sally Hogshead (yes that is really her name ) she details a process for how we can be more fascinating and outlines your seven triggers to be more persuasive and captivating - definitely a great read.

One statement that really impacted me was, "We are networking, not connecting." She went on to say that we're doing things so we can tell others we did them. "We are living hyperlinks!" says Richard Laermer. Wow - what a powerful statement. In his book *Free*, Chris Anderson says, "Hyperlinks are the formal exchange of attention and reputation."

In our digital, hyper-connected world are we missing great opportunities to really connect with people we care about?

The Wizard of Oz said, "A heart is not judged by how much you love, but how much you are loved by others."

People don't want to connect with brands; they want to connect with each other. People want to connect with people. In *Free*, Chris Anderson also says we all have an average of 100 Facebook friends. He goes on to ask the question: can one generation have more attention and capacity than another?

We say, "We don't have time to do everything ... we only have time to do what matters."

Today decide that you will reach out to someone and truly connect with them, have a real conversation, look them in the eye, put down the remote control, get off your iPhone, iPad, Blackberry (whatever your addiction of choice is) and connect.

## Speak Productively: Create a language palette

Want to save time in meetings?

Wish your emails were more concise?

Ever want to move a conversation along so you can focus on the next task?

If you answered yes to any of these questions, then you need to **create a productive language palette**. Just like an artist has a variety of colors for their palette, we can create a linguistic palette that increases productivity through simple phrases.

If you want to **keep a conversation progressing** use a simple phrase, "Let's move on." These three powerful words are not confrontational and send a direct message to progress the conversation.

If you are a **in a meeting** and people are side tracked, try my favorite phrase, "For the sake of time." Then you can combine it with, "Let's move on". This sends a subtle signal to attendees that time is precious, and you have more agenda items to finalize.

In a meeting, **five minutes before finishing** conclude with, "In the five minutes we have left, let's agree on action items." This is another subtle way to remind people of the time and to ensure the meeting has agreed-upon action plans.

To **avoid email 'thank you' back and forth** clogging up your inbox, try this simple closing in your email signature, "Thank you in advance for your help/assistance."

When **someone calls your phone** without an appointment, try this simple greeting, "Great to hear from you, what is on your agenda for our phone call today?" Or, "How can I help you today?" There is no need for small talk, and this friendly greeting allows your caller to get right to the point of the conversation.

**Spin outcomes** – Be a 'master of spin'; find a way to always identify the most positive outcome in all situations and share that – where possible, keep all conversations positive to help them stay productive.

## Eliminate Urgency

Have you ever seen an episode of *The Simpsons*? In one of the episodes, the school psychiatrist is sharing with Homer Simpson, Bart's father, that Bart has trouble with his attention span. Homer is sitting there staring at the psychiatrist saying to himself, "Blah, blah, blah" – it is funny … but sometimes true!

How often when people tell you that something is 'urgent' do you respond with blah, blah, blah? There are words we use in our language palette that don't create the responses we are looking for.

**Eliminate urgent** – When you use words like *ASAP* or *urgent* – people don't pay attention. These words are over-used, and people have become immune to their true meaning.

**Replace urgency with time specific language** – Instead of telling someone a project or task is urgent try this:

"I would appreciate you giving this your highest priority and returning it to me by 4pm today because it is required for a report due at 5pm. This will give me 60 minutes to implement your suggestions."

**Replace Close of business** (a crazy term to begin with) – When someone says, "close of business" to me I wonder, "Whose close of business?" As an Aussie living in the USA, we run two time zones (one for Australia and one for the East Coast where I live). Replace "close of business" with a specific time, i.e., "Can you please get that to me by 4pm today so I can then review it to get it out to my client by 5pm?"

We live and work in a global economy with global triggers. Increase your awareness of global time and folding time by talking specific amounts of time.

## Speak Positively

Allow your words to impact the world. Words have the ability to inspire, motivate or hurt … when you choose to always have a positive language palette you will be more productive and impactful in your conversations.

**Replace Red flag words** – A word to avoid using is 'problem' – this word has the ability to stop a conversation, create conflict and isn't positive. We prefer to use the word 'challenge'. Challenge insinuates that there is a solution, a possible outcome. Try it, replace *problem* with *challenge*.

**Stop 'shoulding' on people** – If someone says to you, "You know what you should do?" – how do you react? The word *should* feels like someone else's expectations; eliminate this red flag word.

**Don't try** – The word 'try' doesn't sound productive. If someone tells you they will "try and attend" your function, you secretly know they won't be there. When you tell someone you will try it doesn't sound confident. It is half-hearted and meaningless, not productive.

**Don't say 'but'** – But is a connector word. No one listens to what you say before the word but, they only hear what you say afterwards. If someone says, "I like your sweater, but is that really the best color for you?" – as the receiver all you hear is "I don't like your sweater." But is often used to connect sentences. Increase your language effectiveness by eliminating the word but (and don't be sneaky and try and replace with this 'however' – it works the same as but).

**Stop saying, "May I pick your brains?"!** – In the Sydney Zoo in Australia there is an amazing gorilla enclosure where you can watch a gorgeous family of gorillas caring for each other. This dreadful phrase reminds me of the gorillas at the zoo picking at each other.  Please eliminate this from your language. It is not productive and often insinuates you want to get free advice or consulting from someone. A better phrase would be, "May I tap into your brilliance?" Now that sounds more productive.

**Change the energy of a room** – When you choose positive language you can defuse situations, and encourage and elevate the conversations in a room.

**Consider your personal brand** – Each of us has words and phrases we use frequently. These words become something we are known for. What words do you use frequently? These words become part of your personal brand. If you want to elevate your personal brand, consider choosing to speak positively.

## Talk time

If you want to increase your language effectiveness, sound productive by talking time. Talking time is using time in your language to achieve results. Talking time increases your own sense of time; it is effective in meetings and during presentations, also.

If you have ever traveled to a country where English is not their first language you will realize the importance of understanding another language. On our first trip to Italy, after leaving Rome, we stayed in an olive grove in Tuscany – a tiny town called Calci where no one spoke English! Before our trip I had studied the language. (Well, I had listened to DVDs in my car … does that count?) Knowing phrases and possible responses allowed us to get around Italy, order food, converse with people in stores (while I didn't know how to respond if people replied) – the locals knew that I was trying and were very helpful.

Talking time will show others around you a deep respect for their time and appreciation of how important time is.

**Choose words wisely about time** – Choose to say, "I didn't choose to spend time on that" instead of, "I don't have time."

**Always Ask a Question** – Often, when consulting to people on how to increase their professional presences, one of the strategies we share is to always ask a strategic question.

If you are in a meeting, in a forum, at a conference or with your mentor … always be prepared to stand up, stand out and always ask a strategic question.

The reasons that make a strategic question such an effective engagement technique is that it will:
- ◀ Increase your knowledge.
- ◀ Build your profile and reputation.
- ◀ Position you as an authority.
- ◀ Build your confidence.
- ◀ Increase your communication skills.
- ◀ Stretch your presentation skills.

These are powerful reasons to always be prepared with a strategic question.

**Be first** – Be prepared with your question and be the first to ask it in a large group. Be bold and confidently introduce yourself and ask your question. Ensure your question is strategic and that the context is big enough that others in the room will benefit from the answer.

While attending a huge meeting industry event  (as a virtual attendee), I tweeted a question to keynote speaker Gary Shapiro (the CEO of the Consumer Electronics Show, one of the largest technology trade shows hosted in Las Vegas every year). Not only did he answer my question brilliantly, he also used my name in his response.

People are willing to help you and engage with you when you invest the time to ask a question, especially if it adds value to the audience and allows the speaker to extend their content.

One of the mentees in our Mentor Program was a senior leader within the pharmaceutical industry. She was attending an industry conference in New York and wanted a strategy to stand out in the crowd; I suggested she prepare a valuable question. She did. The results were amazing, and she also was given a private audience with one of the leading experts in her field. Never underestimate the power of a great question.

To prepare a great question consider the following:

**Research the topic** – Have an idea of the topic being discussed to help craft your question.

**Research the audience** – Understand who is in the room and how they might also benefit from your well-crafted question.

**Research the speaker** – If you are attending an industry conference or event, know a little about the speaker: their bio or books published to know their style and expertise. This will help you to direct your question for a positive response.

**Stand up** – When you are in a large group, please stand up (if possible) so everyone can see and hear you.

**Use the microphone** – If one is on offer, always use it.

**Thank** – After the meeting or presentation is complete, always thank the speaker for answering your question and let them know what you enjoyed about their response.

## Make an Impactful Impression

You have seven seconds to make a first impression – only seven seconds! In that first seven seconds people assess your age, your income, your marital status, your education and your interests! That's crazy.

At 13 years old, while attending a school camp at Mt Tamborine Queensland, Australia, I saw this really cute boy at the front of the auditorium. Of course this was before email and Facebook, and I recall thinking to myself, "Wow he is cute, I think I need to get his phone number." (Remember this is before cell phones, people.) There was something about his smile, fabulous blue eyes, and the way he looked at people so intensely … and he later became my husband – talk about first impressions!

While speaking for MTV Networks in New York, I jumped in the elevator very early in the morning, just me and one other person.  I was professionally dressed (as I was speaking for them that day), and the young lady who joined me was feeling frantic, looked like she had just rolled out of bed and was complaining how early she had to come into work that day. For some reason, I just knew she had to be in our program – imagine her surprise when we got out at the same floor and walked to the same room – funny! You never know when you will make an impression on someone.

If you have ever had the pleasure of meeting my friend Scott Ginsberg, you know he is known as the Nametag Guy. For over 10 years he has been wearing a nametag every day. Yes, that's right, it says, "Hello, my name is Scott." His philosophy of making the world more approachable starts with him. He has made a huge impact on the planet, as he has spoken all over the world, written many books on the topic and is an award winning blogger. One of the things that has always impressed me about Scott is that he is always making an impactful impression on everyone he meets. He makes those first seven seconds so easy for people.

If your company is fortunate enough to have a receptionist, that person is a great representation of your company. The moment someone enters your building they get an impression of you and your company – what do you need to do to make sure that is an impactful impression every time?

# Engagement Tools

## Trap your Thoughts

Have you ever watched a spider spin an elaborate web? The beauty is intriguing - the spider had a system to create it. A spider web is a device built by a spider from proteinaceous spider silk from its spinnerets. (How's that for some trivia?) Insects get trapped in their webs, providing nutrition to the spider. Did you know that not all spiders build webs to catch prey, and some do not build webs at all? Spider web is typically used to refer to a web that is still in use (nice and clean); cobweb refers to abandoned (dusty), webs.

When taking notes, my husband says I draw spider webs. His description is great because if you look at them, they do look like webs with an idea in the middle and branches going in every direction. I use them to trap ideas, just like the spider.

Tony Buzan, author and thought leader in the way the brain works, invented the Mind Map. He shares that the Mind Map is a thinking tool that reflects externally what goes on inside your head.

My spider webs are used to capture ideas, take minutes in meetings, increase creativity, map a new project, outline an article, design a speech - some of my clients call this *Neen-storming*. (A fun version of brainstorming I guess?)

Neen-storming is a way to leverage brilliance, save time and capture and sequence information and ideas.

Mapping your mind is fun; simply start with an idea in the center, then each new thought related to that central idea gets its own branch. Simple. The ideas related to each branch are then an extension of the idea.

To make these even more productive once all the ideas are on the page, I take it a step further and sequence them. This is especially helpful when preparing a speech or writing an article.

When I started my MBA I took traditional linear notes, whatever the professor said, I wrote it down. I did OK, got passes and credits. Half way through my MBA I discovered mind mapping and found I could take one page of notes in a whole class and then my results went from passes and credits to honors and high distinctions – crazy! Finally I had found a way to trap my thoughts and ideas in a way my crazy creative brain could remember them. At the start of each exam I would simply draw the mind map I had studied and voila – questions were answered!

In the late 1950's, Dr. Roger Sperry began his research regarding the brain. Sperry's work (which earned him a Nobel Prize in Medicine in 1981) proved the brain is divided into two major areas: the right and left-brain.  His research also identified that each part of the brain specializes in its own style of thinking and has different capacities.

An easy way to remember this is left is logical and right is creative.  He went on to detail each of these thinking styles and we have listed below the capacities:

| **Left = Logical** | **Right = Creative** |
| --- | --- |
| ◀ Sequential thinking | ◀ Insights |
| ◀ Sees details | ◀ Imagination |
| ◀ Logical cause and effect | ◀ Face Recognition |
| ◀ Language functions/grammar rules | ◀ Spatial orientation |
| ◀ Uses facts | ◀ Drama |
| ◀ Speaks well | ◀ Metaphors |
| ◀ Good with numbers | ◀ Music |
| ◀ Word puzzles | ◀ Meditation/prayer |
| ◀ Analyzes | ◀ Rap/rhyme |
| ◀ Names things | ◀ Art/colours |

## Super-productive people have whole brain thinking.

A great way to increase your creativity and stretch your thinking is to ask questions. Questions can be used for clarification, probing assumptions, probing evidence and reasons, questioning viewpoints and probing consequences.

**Some of my favourite questions to ask include:**
- ◀ **Who** is this for? Who does this affect? Who else would benefit from this?
- ◀ So what?
- ◀ **What** is the story? What is the point? What exactly does this mean? What do we already know about this? What else can we assume? What would happen if we …? What other ways could we look at this? What are the pluses and minuses of…?
- ◀ **Where** is the best place for this? Where do we want this story to go?
- ◀ **When** is this due? When is action required?
- ◀ **How** is this relevant? How is this important? How is this a story? How is this related to other projects/clients? How will that affect …?
- ◀ **Why** do you think that? Why is this happening? Why is this better than …?

If you are looking for strategies to increase your productive creativity try these:
- ◀ Be open.
- ◀ Drive a different way to work.
- ◀ Order an unusual meal.
- ◀ Read magazines (fashion, travel, food).
- ◀ Ask more questions.
- ◀ Visit an art museum.
- ◀ Watch foreign films.
- ◀ Travel abroad.
- ◀ Be well read.
- ◀ Try Neen-storming.
- ◀ Surround yourself with creative people.
- ◀ Take a walk.

I love this quote by Oliver Wendell Holmes: "A mind once stretched by a new idea, never regains its original dimensions." Asking questions, using *Neen-storming* and being more creative will definitely stretch your mind!

## Demonstrate Impactful Integrity

Elizabeth Gilbert, thought leader and author of *Eat, Pray, Love,* says, "Having a baby is like getting a tattoo on your face. You really need to be certain it's what you want before you commit."

Tattoos are a commitment leaving a permanent mark on your body; the combination of commitment, design and color. I love tattoos and do realize they are not for everyone. Each of my many tattoos means something to me. (Surprise, you didn't know I had tattoos did you?) Ink is permanent, forever marking a memory, occasion, loved one or phrase that means something to you.

Just like tattoos, someone with impactful integrity combines personal and professional integrity to change the planet. Do you know someone like this?

Bono, rock star legend and front man of U2, is a great example of someone who has combined his passion and incredible influence to impact the planet. On January 26, 2006 he launched the Product RED campaign. This campaign was designed to raise awareness and funds to help eliminate AIDS in Africa. Products that are licensed under this brand include everything from clothing to iPods, and like many of you reading, I bought many of these products. Beyond the fact that these products are cool, we purchase them knowing the money contributes to a global fund that makes a difference in the lives or people we may never meet.

As the founder of Thought Leaders Global, Matt Church created a movement in Australia and beyond, sharing with people how to capture, package and deliver their expertise into the world using proprietary tools and templates. His passion on helping clever people become commercially smart has had a ripple effect across the planet as global partners opened new markets, and thought leaders were created and began to impact their community. His passion for speaking, writing and teaching changed the way people deliver messages in the world.

Oprah, someone I deeply admire for the way she has changed the planet through her philanthropic focus, created the Angel Network in 1988 after she invited viewers in an episode to join her and use their lives to improve the lives of others. The Angel Network was created to encourage people around the world to make a difference. Oprah had a vision to inspire individuals to enable underserved women and children to rise to their potential.

Peter Sheahan, successful Aussie entrepreneur and CEO in the trenches, is universally known for inspiring innovative business thinking and creating lasting business change. He founded ChangeLabs where he partners with leading brands to creative innovative change programs that transform communities, build brand equity and create competitive advantage. One of the coolest programs Pete has created is The Financial Literacy Skills Program, helping educate over one million young people since its creation.

What can you do to impact the world combining your professional and personal integrity?

## Surround Yourself with VIPs (Very Inspiring People)

A VIP is a very inspiring person. Surround yourself with people who are impressive to you, who inspire you to be better, do better and make the world a better place because you are in it. Spending time with VIPs motivates and invigorates you and ultimately accelerates your productivity.

Spending time with VDPS (very draining people) kills your productivity. Simple – eliminate VDPs and choose only VIPs.

Have you ever eaten a huge meal that looked amazing, but once you had eaten it you regretted your decision? That meal made you feel uncomfortably full and caused you to want to go and take a little nap. That's what VDPs do – they rob you of energy and demotivate you.

When I first moved to Doylestown, PA from Sydney, Australia I reached out to a someone in my industry who lived in my area. and I thought for sure we'd hit it off. And we did … initially. As time progressed and we spent more time together, I realized she was one of the most negative people I had ever met. Her outlook on life was different to mine; she had certainly had her share of challenges, and I have no right to make any assessments about what her attitude should or could be. I found myself dreading our time together, making excuses not to connect with her, until eventually I had to share with her the truth. It was my issue, not hers; however, I found her negativity hard to be around. She was indeed a VDP. Such a shame, I am not proud of this; I hoped my crazy Pollyanna view of the world might rub off on her, but alas it didn't, and so I ended it. It was awkward. Eliminating VDPs in your life is tough and not always possible.

One of the VIPs in my life is my special friend Donavan, mentioned earlier in this book. He has a crazy laugh, is incredibly inquisitive, and when he talks with you he gives you his undivided attention. Rare for a kid his age and yet he is one of the most engaging people I know. Spending time with him is always a treat. If you want more VIPs in your life, look around at the kids you know – their zeal for life and desire to grow will definitely rub off on you.

When you are in control of your time, choose to invest wisely with VIPs only.

## Practice Engagement Mastery

Someone who has mastered engagement is Brian Tracy, prolific author, speaker and all round great man. He says there are three steps to mastery:

◄ Read for one hour every day.

◄ Attend courses and conventions in your area of expertise or industry.

◄ Listen to CDs in your car.

These simple strategies make a lot of sense and yet – why don't we do them?

Successful people continually put pressure on themselves to perform at the highest level.

## Spotlight: Social Media engagement with Gina Schreck

According to a study published in *New Technology, Work and Employment* (and reprinted in *Real Simple* magazine August 2012) workers who take short internet breaks (to check Facebook or read the news) are 9% more productive than employees who barrel through the day with nary a status update or YouTube diversion. The psychologist behind this research surmises that online interludes restore mental capacity and provide a feeling of autonomy which in turn boosts effectiveness.

"Social media is not about you – it's about them," says geeky guru and chief hooligan at Social KNX, Gina Schreck. She also says, "There will always be the 'next thing' in social media, focus on the best place for you and your clients right now."

Do you remember when people said Facebook would never last? Well, it's still here!

As one of the leading experts in social media, Gina's book *Getting Geeky with Twitter* is an excellent resource for those wanting to know how to do social media right. Her firm manages the social media activity for a diverse range of clients across the globe, from small businesses to large hotel chains, and every client will tell you she makes them sound amazing online.

While researching our latest book project, we interviewed this geeky genius to understand how people could be more engaging online.

Gina shared with us that social media has changed our interactions and access. No longer do we need to be concerned about connecting with the media, celebrities or well-known authors and speakers; they are simply a tweet away. Social media has provided greater access to people; it has removed gatekeepers and given everyone a greater sense of boldness when connecting with others.

Here is some of the brilliance she shared with us:

**Be present** – Don't just send a few status updates and assume that your social media presence taken care of. She advised that you need to interact with people, respond to their posts, comment on blogs, like status updates, and re-tweet information. Online is a conversation – there are just more people involved.

**Engage in conversation on multiple platforms** – She recommends visiting profiles of others; don't restrict your activities to one or two social media sites.

**75/25 split** – Focus on others 75% of the time and the remaining 25% you can focus on sharing information about yourself. This requires you to be engaged and present; to be aware of what others are doing and sharing their content and information with others. Don't just broadcast - share.

**Be strategically social** – Get involved in Tweet chats for your industry or client base; make lists online to follow others and develop relationships. Have a plan of who you want to develop relationships with and then seek them out online. People are more likely to accept your invitation to connect on LinkedIn if you have exchanged tweets and Facebook comments, she says.

**Use technology** – One of her recommended apps (and my personal favorite for social media) is HootSuite. This great tool allows you to create columns to follow lists, watch hash tags and post to multiple social media platforms.

**Schedule social time** – Set a goal to reach out to five people each day that you haven't chatted to in a while. Determine what time of day is best for you to visit certain platforms – i.e., Pinterest is busy at night with people enjoying the site while they watch TV or do other activities. People are more social at night and more business-focused during the day, she says. Remember that when you are online. Commit to daily online activity to build your community.

**Blur the lines** – Your offline and online conversations are blurring, so ensure you are your most authentic self and be involved in conversations; bring more of you to the online world.

Have we connected online? Have you been to our Facebook page? Do you follow us on Twitter? Need quick productivity videos to share with your team on YouTube? Want great eye candy on our Pinterest boards or chat on LinkedIn? However you like to connect we'd love to be in an online conversation with you!

What can you do in your practice to engage in more conversations on-line? Where are you focusing your social media attention?

## Be Someone's Hero

Eleanor Roosevelt was the First Lady of the United States from 1933 to 1945 – she was a pretty cool chick. She was not only an advocate for the civil rights movement but she was one of the greatest women of the 20th century. She was a humanitarian, wife of president Franklin D. Roosevelt and an active member of the women's suffrage movement (the right of women to vote and run for office).

She said one of my favorite quotes, "Do one thing every day that scares you."

She was a hero. I bet if I had the opportunity to sit down and chat with her over a latte she would suggest we all help someone become who they want to be. When people recognize their own value they increase it. It is easy to be scared by our own potential, however if you help someone discover it you make an impact!

Could you support two people for every one person that has supported you? Imagine the impact you would have on the planet – now that's folding time!

## Relationship Engagement

**Conscious Celebration -** We always have time to do what matters.

Recently one of my clients celebrated the opening of his new, funky commercial space. I should also tell you, he is one of the top entertainers in the US and is admired and respected within his industry. When Jason throws a party, people come from miles around just to help him celebrate!

When I spoke with other amazingly talented guests (including rock star entertainers Marcello Pedalino and Mike Walter) who were there to share the night with him at his SCE Event Group open house, absolutely everyone was full of praise for him, his team and his commitment to excellence. He was surrounded by the best of the best.

I drove two hours to celebrate with him (which by the way, I would normally think absolutely NO way) and yet, when I received his invitation I didn't even give it a second thought! Other guests drove four hours or more, and this is testimony to him. Of course I also used the drive down to connect with some amazing people by phone (yes on hands-free) … just being productive!

We often hear people say, "I'm too busy." AND we are all busy. My good friend and awesome stylist Megan Kristel says, "I don't believe in being too busy for my people." She believes we always make time for those who are important to us. I agree.

At Jason's open house people were there to congratulate him, connect with others in their industry and they consciously chose to celebrate – how often do you do that in your life? Do you wait until your birthday each year? Do you wait for a public holiday?

Not me! I like to celebrate the little things, the big things and especially the things that matter to others.

The most productive people I know do less, not more … but they do more of the things that energize them.

## Spotlight: Increase Engagement by Focusing on the Environment with Marcello Pedalino

Productivity is more than managing time. True productivity is the combination of how you manage your time, focus your attention and manage your energy. The most productive people I know do less, not more. (Yes, you read that right.) They do more of the things that energize them.

Keeping the attention of others on a daily basis can be a challenge, so recently we interviewed people we admire to ask about the secrets of how they effectively engage people.

One of the successful leaders we interviewed was Marcello Pedalino. He believes in celebrating life and enjoying the journey through this world as much as possible; to "work hard and play hard" is his motto.

From the first moment you meet him you are aware of his undivided attention, genuine smile and exceptional conversational skills. I was fortunate to be part of an invitation-only retreat for top entertainers in the USA, where I met the most fascinating people. This group of award winning entertainers considers it their calling to provide experiences for people that they will treasure for a lifetime.

When asking Marcello how he engages people, he shared, "By smiling and being as polite as possible." This seems obvious, right? Then why don't more leaders do this? He continued to share that if the situation demands more than just "good manners and genuine eye contact," the next strategy is to **gain control of the surroundings that directly affect people's sensory system**.

He shared that when his company provides the entertainment, production and hospitality for an event, they make sure guests are comfortable throughout the celebration. Guests who are comfortable are in a good mood … if they are in a good mood, they are happy. **Happy people are extremely receptive to taking verbal direction, getting involved and following your lead**.

Smell, hearing, sight, and temperature are all essential elements of comfort. When people smell tantalizing aromas, listen to the perfect song at the right volume, look at a well-groomed performer or event host in a beautifully decorated space, and their body temperature is like Goldilocks' porridge, **they are extremely receptive to engagement from an effective conversationalist** … especially one who knows how to adjust oratory delivery accordingly based on the demographic and personalities in the room.

It made me wonder, as leaders, how could we create more comfortable environments for our teams to ensure they are fully engaged in the everyday business? What could you do to engage your team more and accelerate their productivity? What could you do to focus more of your attention on people you care about when you are at home?

We don't have time to do everything; we only have time to do what matters. Invest time today by engaging with someone who matters to you.

## Spotlight: Demonstrate Personal Integrity with Stacey Hanke

Do you have someone in your life that demonstrates the highest level of personal integrity? For me, one of those people is a thought leader in the area of influence, Stacey Hanke.

As the founder and CEO of Stacey Hanke, Inc., she works with executives around the world to increase their influence and impact through communication skills. She is engaging, high energy and always on purpose. With a crazy travel schedule for her clients (that would kill a normal person), her level of stamina and commitment to her practice is admired by many. Stacey's strategies for increasing accountability and engagement include:

**Know why you do what you do** – Be clear on why you get up every day and share your message with the world. This clarity will help drive your decisions and communications.

**Know why you say what you say** – Plan conversations carefully; be prepared for each conversation to be focused on how you can help the other person. Think strategically about the words you use, your eye connection and your body language.

**Know what your top priorities are** – Each day on a post-it note write your absolute must do's that day, then get them done. Carry it with you until completed – it will keep you focused. If something is not a priority, pass on it or pass it along to someone who can help you.

**Apply Neen's 15-minute rule** – Stacey shared that this concept changed her conversations and awareness of making the most of all the minutes we have in a day.

**Create accountability discipline** – Work with a coach, use a mastermind group and avoid distractions. Stay clearly focused on your next 90-day plan to avoid overwhelm. Know what is important to you and why, and then share that with someone to help you achieve it and keep you honest.

## Spotlight: Purposeful Engagement with Kim Woodworth

Have you ever met someone that had such a positive impact on you that you constantly explored opportunities to meet with them, learn from them and partner with them? When I first met Kim Woodworth, an executive at Comcast Spotlight, that's what happened to me. She is high energy, engages everyone around her and is deeply admired by her peers and her team. She demonstrates exceptional engagement skills, and we interviewed her to learn how she does it. Here is a summary of how she purposely engages with people daily:

**Choose the right people** – Look closely at those you hire and ensure they will fit in both your culture and your company. Surround yourself with the right people to achieve the objectives of your company.

**Work hard to remind people** – Constantly remind people that they matter to the project or team you are part of. Go out of your way to seek people out on a daily basis and let them know their actions have impacted the project or delighted a customer or helped the team achieve their objectives.

**Create energy** – Taking care of your health through exercise, diet and sleep ensures when you meet with people you present the best version of yourself. Take responsibility for your energy levels and the way you engage those around you by focusing on sleeping deeply (preferably for seven hours), eating carefully and exercising regularly.

**Remove distractions** – Determine which activities are distracting you from focusing on people and conversations and create systems to eliminate those distractions. Distraction can be thoughts, feelings or physical items. Consider leveraging online bill paying so you aren't distracted by money tasks; employ cleaners for your home so you aren't distracted by feelings of guilt about your environment; leverage technology so you aren't distracted by tools that don't work properly.

**Make happiness and joy a priority** – Choose to turn up in your workplace every day with a feeling of joy. If you have areas of your life that are creating unhappiness, take action to change that. The example Kim shared was sometimes there are areas of our home that remind us life is overwhelming or chaotic (like a fridge that needs cleaning out … every time you see it you are reminded that it needs to be done) – her advice: choose to take action now so you can engage with others more effectively and not be distracted by things that cause unhappiness.

**Say no and be OK** – Decline invitations that aren't appealing to you so you can be free to totally enjoy the activities where you are totally engaged. We have mentioned in previous chapters the power and productivity of the word no and how to say no nicely – consider this an engagement strategy.

People are doing more than they need to do, and people will give you more than you ask, as long as you appreciate them and engage with them authentically each time you connect.

How can you be more engaging in your everyday communications?

**Spotlight: Conversation with Ralph Roberts, Comcast Cable founder**

In the summer of 2010 I was fortunate to be part of a small group of 10 people (employees of Comcast who were also studying at Villanova University) and Mr. Roberts (as he is affectionately and always called within Comcast) shared lessons he had learned in his very successful career.

To be more engaging he shared with us the following suggestions:
- ◀ You need to be able to laugh at yourself often.
- ◀ You need a sense of humor.
- ◀ You need to get people to think like you.
- ◀ Don't be arrogant or proud.
- ◀ Don't be afraid to speak your mind.

He went on to share that the qualities of a leader include those who are optimistic, believe in what you are doing and don't be afraid to learn from someone else.

This exclusive time with Mr. Roberts was treasured by all those in the room.

## Spotlight Bruce White from Johnson Kendall Johnson

One of our favorite clients is Johnson Kendall Johnson (JKJ). We were really impressed with one of the partners of this firm, Bruce White.

This award winning full-service insurance brokerage and risk management firm has managed corporate and personal needs since 1959. Bruce White is someone I admire for his level of incredible engagement with his team, his peers, his family, and his community. He is highly regarded by his peers, admired by his team and loved by his family. We spent some time interviewing him about the productivity challenges of his industry and how he manages to engage people by investing his time and attention with them. We have shared some of his brilliance below:

Bruce shared the biggest challenge of the insurance industry is recruiting talent. He shared it's not a sexy industry, no one grows up saying they want to be in the insurance industry; however, some schools now include risk management in their curriculum. People who are part of this industry, and especially his firm, really care about people.

The insurance industry has been affected by technology in a big way; the data still is entered into a system and then a model assesses risk, etc. It used to be manual, and now technology has provided a great resource to the insurance industry. Health care laws affect insurance – technology and regulation all impact the way we deliver services to our clients, he said.

I laughed when he shared that three words to sometimes describe the industry are: 'male, pale and stale.' Bruce is committed to recruiting high quality people and training them.

When asked about how he **maximizes his productivity** for every day, he had some great ideas including:

**Goal set** – set goals and stick to them. This might mean extending the day or working in between appointments; however, whatever you set out to achieve – make it happen.

**Break down time** – Choose to break it down into 30-minute increments (sometimes even 15 minutes) to get it all done.

**Stay efficient**– Leverage technology all day when possible.

**Make it work!** – Just do whatever it takes, no excuses.

When asked about how he engages people, the strategies he shared included:

**Enjoy people** – Enjoy their stories; he spends hours listening to someone share about their life. He remembers their story and feels emotion from their story. Story is everything – it shows how people get to where they are. Bruce loves to know as much as he can because he cares about who people are and what makes them tick. If you ever are fortunate enough to watch him interact with his team or a client this is very evident.

**Choose to engage** - When we asked how he learned to be more engaging he shared that when he was a kid he was uncomfortably shy, and his recollection was that he didn't want to be that person, so in middle school he decided he wasn't going to be that person. Bruce decided he wasn't going to be too sensitive. His parents taught him to be a gentleman, and he decided he didn't want to be the shy guy on the sidelines - he wanted to step into the forefront of things.

**Provide a forum for people** - Listen so they feel good. Be more engaging when you are listening to clients. People need to spend time listening and not just 'sell' – choose a different pace in the conversation.

**Listen intently** – Give people your full attention, and you will hear their story.   In all professions, especially sales, we need to be a powerful listener so audience engagement increases.

When asked about how he juggles so many competing priorities he shared his strategies to manage:

**Emotional emergency is a priority** – A client issue might be pressing, i.e., contract; however, if an individual human has an emotional issue (team member or family or a friend) – that will always be the priority. Sometimes you can handle things at the same time, but often you might have to go to 'plan b', explain you are not available at the moment for a client but will pass it along to someone else who can help them – you need to be able to deal with things simultaneously.

**Client activity first** – Nothing happens unless we respond to clients well. Bruce shared that he works for JKJ, but he really works for the client. I loved his comments that, "Our business exists because we support our clients to achieve their mission first. **Be internally managed by externally focused**."

**Hire people to keep us focused** – We choose team members to help us stay both internally and externally focused. People are clear on their roles in helping us achieve our mission, and the missions of our clients.

**Always ask, "How can I help you grow your business?"** – He believes in helping people grow, loves meeting new people and thinking about who he can introduce them to, who he can help. This is a great perspective to keep at the forefront of our minds daily – how can we help and whom do we know that others need to know?

**Love to-do lists** – He uses to-do lists so as to not forget things. Easy technology to create tasks, i.e., Outlook – allows notes to be placed in calendar appointments to know what needs to be completed.

**Diary things** – Use calendar to diarize and then check the appointments that are things you need to achieve in the day.

**Leave yourself messages** – Send yourself emails to remember things.

**Write notes in a book** – Bruce shared for every year he has been out of school since 1984 he has notes from every meeting. Like many of our clients, the way he learns is to write it down. Sometimes it is just jotting down a word or a book to read, it is a great way to remember things.

**Be yourself** – Never try and be anything you are not. Just be you. When having a conversation with someone feel what they are feeling, put yourself in their position; look at everyone the same – imagine what they experience. Just always be who you are, but don't be anything except who you are - love this advice.

It was a pleasure to interview Bruce, and he had some great ideas on how to be more engaging.

## action plan

Who is someone you admire that demonstrates exceptional engagement? Write their name here:

_____

Make an appointment to interview them for 15 minutes by phone.
**Ask them, "How do you use engagement in your personal and professional life?"**

Write their responses here: _____

_____

_____

_____

_____

_____

Now what will you do differently as a result of reading this chapter? _____

_____

_____

_____

- **Repurpose everything.**
- **Create once, use often.**
- **Apply the 90/10 rule.**
- **Schedule a weekly review of your success.**
- **Overcome personal gravity.**
- **Conduct a self-audit.**
- **Schedule activity, recovery and re-energy time.**
- **Hire a business manager.**
- **Conduct a time audit.**
- **Leverage everything you do, write and share.**
- **Think once and leverage often.**
- **Barter time and brilliance.**
- **Maintain a healthy focus for energy management.**
- **Visualize your own fabulousness.**
- **Wake up productive (and stay that way).**
- **Practice sleep hygiene.**
- **Use your off-switch.**
- **Get a mentor, be a mentor, be a great mentee.**
- **Be a super-productive connector.**
- **Know your impact.**

# "The world belongs to the energetic."

- Ralph Waldo Emerson

## Repurpose everything: Create once use often

**Apply the 90/10 Rule** – The Italian economist Vilfredo Pareto is famous for creating what has become known as the 80/20 rule. His discovery was that 80% of Italy's land was controlled by 20% of the population. He was then able to apply this formula to so many areas.  The 90/10 rule could be an extension of this theory.

Have you ever worked on a project and it felt like you had to invest 90% to get the last 10% completed? This theory is especially important when it comes to executing and leveraging everything we do.

We need to invest significant attention and energy to increase impact. We make regular choices to do this.

There is a biblical principle called tithing. In the Old Testament of the Bible, Israelites were required to take care of the Levites. They were challenged to tithe (or to donate or give away) to the storehouse.  Later in the Bible an amount of 10% was attached to this commandment.

Much has been written on tithing and the impact it can have on everyday attitude and abundance.  Having been exposed to this principle early in life, it remains high on our annual goals – we set a tithe goal yearly that then dictates financial goals.

In the *One Minute Millionaire* by Mark Victor Hansen and Robert G. Allen they suggest that enlightened millionaires tithe 10%.

The late Dr. Stephen Covey said, "10% of life is what happens to you; 90% of life is decided on how you react."

Much has been said about the 90/10 rule; however, leaders need to know that sometimes you have to invest 90% to get the last 10% complete.

**Schedule a weekly review of your results and successes** – Have you considered taking a few moments each Sunday to review your progress and ensure you are on track and to determine where your highest priorities are for this week? One of the women in our mentoring program now invests 15 minutes every Sunday to set up her week, review the progress of projects from the previous week and remind herself of the successes she had – this powerful activity can create great momentum when you find yourself overwhelmed or crazy busy.

**Leverage social media tools** – If you are engaged online in conversation through social media, you can use tools designed to help you create one post and apply it to multiple platforms. Apps such as HootSuite or other cross platform tools allow you to post once, share everywhere.  Save time using tools instead of going to every website and reposting the same information multiple times.

## Overcome Personal Gravity

**Conduct a self-audit** – Spend time with yourself and identify where you waste time so you can eliminate, delegate or designate to someone else. This self-audit can also include knowing your strengths, determining where you enjoy spending most of your time and areas you wish to avoid spending time on. A great resource in the area of understanding your strengths is *StrengthsFinder 2.0* by Tom Rath. This small book allows you to conduct an online audit to identify your top five strengths and outlines ideas for actions – definitely worth reading to help you with your self-audit.

**Hire a Business Manager** – If you are running a practice that can fund a business manager this will be a huge asset to your team and personal productivity.  In the Thought Leaders community we share a great model that outlines three roles of a practice: **make-up**, **set-up** and **clean-up**.  It explains that in every practice the role of **make-up** is for the person with subject matter expertise. The expert is typically a consultant, speaker, author, trainer, mentor, facilitator or coach (ideally a combination of all of these).  The role of **set-up** is for the business manager: set up meetings, contracts and operational focus for their role. The role of **clean-up**, once your practice is highly profitable, is the Executive Assistant of the Business Manager – yes, you read it right, not your assistant but theirs! Our Business Manager Maria is the key to the operational success of our practice, and my job as a thought leader is to think, sell and deliver.

Could you hire a business manager for your practice?

**Conduct a Time Audit** – Choose one activity you believe you are potentially spending too much time on or wasting time with (i.e., social media), and then log how many minutes/hours you spend on this one activity. The results might scare you. I once tried a social media ban for a week – I only lasted a few hours before being tempted to check in. It was at that point I realized I had a social media addiction and had to be more strategic in my time spent online.

Are you aware of activities where you might be wasting time?

**Schedule Activity, Recovery and Re-energy -** Maximum capacity requires forward planning.

Do you get frustrated when you forget to recharge your cell phone and it dies on you in the middle of a conversation or during your busy day? We say all kinds of crazy things to our phone, desperately hoping it will miraculously have just enough battery life to get us through the teleconference or to the place we are going using the GPS. Forgetting to recharge our own batteries has huge consequences on our personal productivity.

We lead busy lives full of projects, activities and obligations. Most of us have no trouble in scheduling activities – in fact, many of us schedule too many activities! Where we struggle is forgetting to schedule recovery time.

Nature gives us brilliant examples of recovery. A caterpillar, once it grows to approximately one and a quarter inches long, curls into a J-shape and is ready to create a chrysalis. Attaching itself to a leaf or a branch, it curls up and has a little nap for about 10 days. Then it slowly emerges as the butterfly who has a life span of between two to four weeks. As humans we need to curl up sometimes and recover to emerge more energized.

Several years ago, I was part of the National Speakers Association of Australia (NSAA) and co-chaired their annual conference. We had 12 months of planning to support and schedule 350+ speakers from around the world, while attempting to keep everyone happy (Can you imagine organizing an event for speakers? They are constantly exposed to some of the best minds, best venues and best practices. Imagine being the speaker at a speaker's convention!). My co-chair gave me great advice; he said, "Make sure you schedule recovery time." Leading up to the event I wasn't aware of what he meant; however, the morning I woke up after it was all finished – I was exhausted. I had planned one day of recovery, but that wasn't wise – more time was required.

Do you need to schedule recovery time after a major project delivery?

You would think I would have learned my lesson but when agreeing again to co-chair an event for the National Speakers Association (NSA) in the USA (again, maybe I had temporary insanity), I stupidly didn't implement the wisdom given to me all those years ago. After an exhausting 12 months of planning, we had scheduled clients the days after the conference which involved significant travel. If you can visualize a walking zombie – that was the result.

Even when we know we have big projects coming to a close we often neglect to schedule recovery time to allow our body and mind to slow down, recharge and get ready for the next big project.

When we relocated from Sydney, Australia to Doylestown, Pennsylvania, we moved next door to a fantastic all American family with parents who really enjoy each other and three busy, active boys. When the boys were younger we created a Friday night tradition of having dinner together most weeks. Their mum worked every other weekend so sometimes we were fortunate to have her company and other times it was just 'the boys.' These nights became a highlight in our week, and it also changed the way the office managed the calendar.

Spending time with kids is so energizing; they don't need or want anything from you but your undivided attention. (Well, that is the opinion of someone who isn't a mother.) I guess you could say they became our substitute children.

Our calendar was structured to ensure that no matter where we were speaking or flying, whenever possible we would be home by 5pm on Fridays to have dinner with 'the boys.' This wonderful tradition became re-energizing time.

What do you do that re-energizes you?

## Leverage absolutely everything you say, write and share
**Think once and leverage often.**
If you have invested time in creating a speech, save it and determine if you can turn it into an article for your industry or a training session for a team member. When you write instructions for a new process, determine if you can create a training call with other team members to share it, or if you can create an article from it to share on your intranet.

**Barter time and brilliance: Repurpose others' expertise**
The barter system has been around since the beginning of man. While there may not have been currency we assume that people traded items they needed with each other to survive. People would exchange personal possessions that were perceived to be valuable for something they needed, i.e., livestock, shells.

Regardless of your financial situation you can barter time and brilliance.

When relocating to the USA, I had absolutely no clients and no income, so I had to be creative in the way we established products and services needed. We needed book keeping services to establish systems, so we bartered with a financial controller to help her increase the productivity of her and her team, and she helped with accounts.

What skills do you have that you can barter with someone else?

**Barter your expertise**

If you are a PowerPoint whiz but hate Excel spreadsheets, can you barter time with someone who has a specialty in that area? Many of our clients do this now, and they are focused on doing more of what they love and trading their time for those activities they enjoy the least.

What skills do you offer the world?

## Energy management: Maintain a Healthy focus

Productivity means managing your energy – music accelerates that!

Clients, friends and family often ask, "How do you stay so energized?" They also often ask, "Are you always like this?" My reply: "Yes, my poor husband!"

Running a thought leadership practice, managing a large corporate team or managing a family requires stamina. Like all of you reading this, we have crazy busy lives, and one of the most important activities we can do to boost our energy is to exercise – OK, I heard you all groan!

This is not a chapter about how to exercise because honestly … it is absolutely NOT my favorite thing to do; however, there are many ways to make it more fun, and I hope some of these might inspire you to increase your energy, too.

**Hire a trainer** – I know … it costs money AND it is worth every cent! The high level of accountability and having to show up is reason enough. Big shout out to Ed Allen, trainer at Fitness Together, who makes me work harder than I even think possible! If you can't afford a trainer, recruit a buddy to kick your butt and workout together! If you want to increase your accountability, share it online like our friend Cynthia D'Amour (who at the time of writing had already lost 85 pounds) who has shared her fitness journey with us all online – inspirational!

**Play groovy running music** – This is really the trick behind my treadmill time. I don't love the treadmill; truthfully I think it is silly to walk inside when I live in such a pretty area. However, I choose it because of air conditioning, and because I don't want my neighbors to be subjected to my off-key singing. Yep, you read it right. My husband begs me not to sing when I am out and about. (Let's just say he is being kind and hoping to prevent my embarrassment).  He also doesn't enjoy it when I bop around the house with my iPod on singing at the top of my lungs … or singing when we are in the car together!  After 24+ years of marriage my voice and singing hasn't improved.

**Create a 30-minute playlist –** This is key: create a list that allows 30 minutes workout and a cool down to your favorite boppy songs.  If you work out for 45 minutes, create that – you get the idea. It helps you stay focused to complete your workout.

**Visualize your own fabulousness** – While singing out loud (way too loud according to my honey) and bopping on the treadmill, can you picture yourself acting out the songs?

Is that crazy? I was the little girl who sang ABBA songs into her hairbrush! I might sound crazy, but when hearing *California Girls* by Katy Perry I imagine friends laughing and walking along Santa Monica Pier. When hearing *Party Rock Anthem* I imagine my cool friend and DJ extraordinaire Jason Jani spinning the tunes on stage while Marcello Pedolino is rocking with the crowd, and I am bopping on the dance floor. Admitting all this to you all might affirm for you all what a crazy place my imagination is – insane maybe – visualizing myself having fun instead of the boring treadmill is far more fun for me! Your imagination can take you anywhere!

**Work out when you wake up** –Don't put it off. Place your workout clothes beside your bed so as soon as you wake you can pull them on and head out for a walk, to the gym or to your own home gym. Working out early gets it out of the way and starts your day energetically. You can easily make excuses for not exercising later in the day. Get it done early, no interruptions, no excuses – do it.

*Real Simple* magazine did a survey in 2011 of 3,250 American women aged 25-54 about free time. Some of you reading this don't understand the concept of free time – you have none!

One of the findings was that the never-ending to-do lists aren't just bad for our psyches and relationships, they are bad for our physical health. Our bodies release a stress hormone called cortisol (always remember cortisol makes you cranky) and high cortisol levels have been linked to burn out.

It's not just what we choose to do with our free time or even the amount of free time that matters. Sociologists Liana Sayer at The Ohio State University in Columbus, Marybeth Mattingly at the Carsey Institute at the University of New Hampshire in Durham, and Suzanne Bianchi at the University of California, Los Angeles have all found that women's free time is more likely to be contaminated, fragmented and interrupted than men's. "Contaminated time" refers to leisure activities that are combined with something else, frequently housework or childcare.

One of the most significant findings to come out of the sociology research is that, owing to all this contamination and fragmentation, free time for women may be ineffectual – meaning it may not give the real opportunity to take a breath and recharge batteries. What is more disconcerting about this is that the time pressure experienced by married women appears to be self-imposed. 64% of women surveyed felt that if they did less around the house, they would feel as if they weren't taking care of it properly. The article continued to say, "Women still feel that they are going to be held accountable if the housework and the child care don't get done."

Our bodies need recovery time; they need to recover physiologically after work.

## Wake-Up Productive (and stay that way)

While researching this book, we interviewed an expert in the area of medical education and thought leader Karen Roy on how we could wake-up productive. Here are the strategies she shared:

"You can wake up productive and know how to manage your circadian sleep-wake cycle and stay that way!" says Karen Roy.

A great day starts with a great night's sleep; ensure you get the right amount of quality sleep. We refer to Sleep Hygiene, a series of habits to encourage the best night's sleep possible.

**Sleep hygiene** (more than clean sheets, but that's not a bad idea either).

**Create the ideal sleep environment** - Make sure that the environment is pleasant and relaxing. The bed should be comfortable, the room not be too hot or cold or too bright. Black out lining on curtains is a great idea to block out light, especially if you live in an urban environment where streetlights and traffic mean it never gets truly dark outside.

**Travel tip -** Carry a bulldog clip with you so you can pin the curtains closed and keep the light out.

**Associate your bed with sleep** - Experts will tell you the only activities that belong in bed are sleep and sex.  It's not a good idea to use your bed to watch TV, listen to the radio or read excessively.   Do not bring work to bed.

**Try to avoid too much technology in the bedroom** - It's not only bad feng shui but there is an emerging field of research on the negative effects of smartphones in the bedroom – the electrical signals they send out even while on a standby mode may disturb sleep.

Did you know the use of smartphones late at night can delay the onset of sleep simply because you have not switched off from the day's events?

**Prepare for sleep** - In Karen's house, she calls it "windy downy time", and it is just that - winding down from the day to prepare for restful, restorative sleep.

**Establishing a regular relaxing bedtime routine** can make a huge difference.  If watching TV (ideally not in bed), be sure to lower the lights and sound and don't watch something too stimulating.  Try to avoid emotionally upsetting conversations and activities before trying to go to sleep.  Try not to dwell on or bring your problems to bed.

Preparing for sleep starts earlier than you might think.  We need to avoid stimulants and stimulating behaviors hours before sleep time to stack the odds in favor of sleeping well.

**Avoid stimulants** - Such as caffeine, nicotine and alcohol too close to bedtime.  While alcohol is well known to speed the onset of sleep, it disrupts sleep in the second half of the night as the body begins to break down the alcohol, causing arousal.

**Timing your exercise routine is important** - Exercise can promote good sleep and is recommended; however, **vigorous exercise should be taken in the morning** or late afternoon, at the latest, to avoid delaying sleep onset. A relaxing exercise, like yoga, however, can be done before bed to help initiate a restful night's sleep.

Food can be disruptive right before sleep too, so try **to avoid heavy meals close to bedtime**. Also, try to remember the caffeine content in certain foods can be stimulating and avoid those late in the evening.

Now that you have laid the foundations for sleep, the most important thing to do is **make time for sleep.**

In today's 24/7 society, it is too easy and tempting to curtail our sleep time in favor of doing something else. We have been led to believe it is a sign of strength to be able to function without sleep (Margaret Thatcher famously claimed to function on four hours a night), but the data now emerging on sleep restriction tells us that this scenario is unlikely for the vast majority of us and that there are also a number of consequences of sleep restriction beyond feeling tired the next day.

It is recommended that healthy adults sleep seven to nine hours each day.

What is your number? How much sleep do you need to function effectively?

In 2010, 30% of civilian employed US adults (40.6 million workers) reported getting less than six hours on average. Night/shift workers fare even worse, with 44% reporting short sleep duration.

In recognition of the importance of adequate sleep to public health *Healthy People 2020* is a government initiative that includes an objective to, "Increase the proportion of adults who get sufficient sleep."

So what are the potential effects of sleep restriction?

- ◀ Impaired cognitive function.
- ◀ Loss of productivity at work.
- ◀ Increased chances of road traffic accidents.
- ◀ Increase weight gain.
- ◀ Lower sex drive.
- ◀ Negative impact on emotional well-being.

It is important to **be consistent** and **develop a regular sleep schedule** as far as possible. The negative effects of sleep restriction on performance can be cumulative.

Burning the candle at both ends in the working week can mean that by the time your day off rolls around, you are impaired as if you have stayed up all night!  It is important to note that we can't necessarily catch up and that reduced performance may linger after a night of recovery sleep.

We also know that **more is not always better** when it comes to sleep.

People who sleep more than the seven to eight-hour average have a significant reduction in lifespan.

Have you ever heard of sleep drunkenness? It's not what you might think.

Excess sleep may be associated with **sleep drunkenness** or sleep inertia which impairs performance upon awakening. This can be an important issue in situations that demand continuous alertness or when you need to be up and running quickly.

Understanding a little about the natural sleep-wake cycle **can help you plan to be most productive throughout the day**.  We naturally have two dips, or times when our drive to wakefulness is at its lowest.  One is in the middle of the night, and you will know the second as the afternoon slump.

So, how do we manage our wakefulness during the day, especially to remain productive in the slump hours?

**Use stimulants strategically** – Caffeinated beverages can help here (but be careful not to extend this too far into evening – caffeine has a long half-life, meaning it can have lasting effects).  If you are a coffee junkie, know how much caffeine you are consuming.  The amount of coffee in any high street coffee house can vary enormously.  If you are not a coffee lover, there are also caffeinated soft drinks easily available and even caffeine gum is available now.

However, one of the **most natural ways to stimulate the brain is light**.  Getting outside in daylight, and walking around for a few minutes can be a powerful countermeasure to the slump.  If you can't get outside, make sure you have decent, bright lighting where you work.  Just as blocking light at night can help us sleep better, enhancing light when we want to be productive is beneficial.

**Wake up at the same time daily** – Ever tried to 'sleep in' on a weekend? Our bodies have an internal alarm clock; you will be more productive if you try to keep the same wake time daily.

**Use your off-switch** – When we first got married, we chose not to have a television for the first few years of our marriage. As newlyweds, you can imagine we had other ways to fill our time.  With busy careers, part-time study and a full social calendar we didn't miss the television. We consciously chose activities that were more engaging.

Today, many years and way too many TV hours later, we reminisce about those early days.  To be more productive requires the use of the off switch, not just for TV, but also for every other device and distraction we have allowed to enter our lives.

To maintain healthy relationships and manage your energy you will need to use the off switch. Here are a few ways you can do that:

**Silent meals** – No we don't mean not talking; turn all phones to silent (or preferably off) during meal times. We admit, we have been known to check text messages or answer a call during dinner; however, this is so unnecessary and also disrespectful to the gorgeous person you are dining with.

**Don't bail because of work** – Have you ever been stood-up by a friend because of work commitments? No one likes this feeling. Where possible, try not to bail on your friends because of work. You need to balance work energy with friend energy to top up reserves and be your most productive self.

The famous philosopher Dolly Parton once said, "Figure out who you are and then do it on purpose" – good advice. We need to be more purposeful in our conversations so we can maintain high energy and strong relationships.

**Get a Mentor: Mentors Accelerate Momentum** - Locate and learn from a mentor to increase your results over time.

The Greek storyteller Homer tells of Odysseus, the King of Ithaca. In this tale, Odysseus asked his friend Mentor to watch over his son Telemachus while he fought in the Trojan War. Mentor was a faithful friend of Odysseus who was left behind.

Many actors will share their mentors, including:
- ◄ Anthony Hopkins credits Laurence Oliver.
- ◄ The late Heath Ledger credited Mel Gibson.

Even Luke Skywalker had a mentor, Obi-Wan Kenobi.

When first contemplating a career as a speaker, I searched Australia and New Zealand for the best speaker available; wanting someone who ran a profitable business, was ethical and loved their family were my requirements — then we discovered Matt Church. I pestered him for nearly six months to mentor me, and he said no many times. (I must have finally worn him down or maybe he was sick of emails, phone calls.)  He agreed to a mentoring relationship for 12 months, and during that time I did whatever possible to learn from him. I traveled with him, attended presentations, worked in his business, sold books at the back of the room and whatever else it was possible to do to watch and learn. Matt's investment probably saved us at least five years in my practice. He was generous with his time, attention and energy.  We would later go on to be involved in joint projects, model creation and later business partnership. He is by far the most impactful mentor I have ever had, and I still seek his advice and guidance today – all these years later – so you can imagine my delight when he agreed to write the foreword in this book.

**Join a mentoring program**
The senior leadership team of a huge pharmaceutical company presented one of the women in our mentoring program to me. They complained she talked too much, had way too many slides when she presented, didn't look like an executive and had no polish. Wow – what a list. We worked together for five months and during that time we worked on her communication skills; she worked with an image consultant in our team, and guess what … within six months she was promoted to a very senior position. Mentors can save you enormous time and accelerate your development.

**Mentors Accelerate**
**If you want to accelerate – hire a mentor.**
**Stalk a mentor.**

**Have a written agreement.** Put your mentoring agreement in writing by outlining each person's responsibilities and commitments. This doesn't have to be a formal agreement; however, documenting both parties' understanding will ensure you focus on the most important aspects of the relationship.

**Set a time limit.** Limit your formal mentoring relationship to six months. This gives you a timeframe within which to achieve your goals and learning.

**Meet monthly.** Make a regular time (that is convenient for your mentor) for a one-hour meeting each month. Plan to meet in a location that suits your mentor, whether it is his or her office, favorite coffee shop or some other place they suggest.

**Set an agenda for each meeting**. Keep an ongoing list of things you would like to discuss with your mentor as issues arise throughout the month. Let your mentor know what you would like to discuss, what challenges you have been facing and what questions you have a few days in advance. If you can't meet in person, book a teleconference and run the meeting in the same way as you would if you were face-to-face.

**Do your homework**. Your mentor might give you activities to try or challenges for the next month – always complete these tasks and report back on your success.

**Promote your mentor to others** . Always take the opportunity to let others know about your mentor's skills, achievements and successes.

**Thank your mentor with the gift of service**. Being a good mentee is all about serving your mentor to create opportunities through which you can draw from their experience – offer to assist them with a project, help out in their business unit, drive them to an event or take them to the airport.

**Do your homework on your mentor** .Find out what your mentor likes to listen to, what books they read, which movies they enjoy and details about their family. This helps you to find areas of common ground where you can deepen your relationship and also to thank them in ways that are important to them.

**Maintain confidentiality.** Keep discussions between you and your mentor private. Never disclose details of your discussions with others.

**Avoid contacting your mentor outside of agreed times.** If you agree to meet once a month save discussions for this meeting. If you do need to contact them outside of this time, use email so that you don't interrupt their daily activities.

**Try to out-do your mentor.** Learn from their experiences but always try and develop your own work that is even better than your mentor's. If you are successful, you could share your new ideas with them and add value by improving their business.

## Be a Super-Productive Connector

When it comes to connecting with the people who matter most, it is our productivity that determines our success.

Whether you want to build your business or climb the corporate ladder, you must be super-productive to reach your goal. The good news is that achieving more doesn't mean doing more! Super-productive connecting takes just minutes a day and provides rewards beyond measure.

A network of quality connections provides a strong foundation for our personal and professional lives. Yet many of us find ourselves so busy that we only half-heartedly attempt to make and maintain rewarding connections. We know that building relationships is a springboard to success, but we just can't seem to find time to cultivate and keep them.

This is where super-productivity comes in. Fortunately, super-productivity is not about doing more; it is not about putting in longer hours or making longer lists. Rather, super-productivity is about focus: focusing your time, focusing your attention and focusing your energy. When you concentrate on relationship-building tactics that create a positive impact you can stop being busy and start achieving. In other words, you can become a super-productive connector.

## Why Super-productive Connecting?

As a busy professional, you probably find that there are not enough hours in the day. Given the competing demands you must juggle, you might find yourself burning the midnight oil or taking work home. The simple truth is you are not going to get to all the items on your lengthy to-do list, but that's OK because you can make the most of the limited time you do have by doing less of the things that aren't important and more of the things that are, including building fabulous relationships.

When you focus your time, attention and energy on becoming a super-productive connector, you will:

- ◀ Enjoy deeper relationships.
- ◀ Grow your business.
- ◀ Advance your career.
- ◀ Enjoy a better quality of life.
- ◀ Add value to those around you.
- ◀ Build your reputation.
- ◀ Increase your professional profile.
- ◀ Have the pleasure of reconnecting with friends, colleagues and family members.

## Getting There from Here: Focusing Your Time and Attention

Firstly, let's talk about budgeting. Just as you budget your finances you need to budget your time to allow for connecting with others. Your first allotment should be enough time – 30 minutes or so – to make a list of the top people with whom you would like to connect or reconnect. You will find the time you spend connecting more rewarding if you focus on this group of people.

Next, set aside 15 minutes each morning to decide who you would like to contact that day, and the best way to do so. Who prefers e-mail and who would most appreciate a handwritten note or a little surprise like a gift certificate to a favorite coffee shop? Keep in mind that in the age of electronic communication, picking up the phone has become a personal touch. Accordingly, consider leaving voicemails for friends, clients and colleagues late at night on their office lines so they are greeted the next morning by your pleasant voice, reminding them that you were thinking of them.

You will also need to schedule time to follow up on your initial contact. I must take this opportunity to stress the importance of follow-up; did you know less than one percent of people follow up on their networking efforts? Be in that minority and take action. For follow-up, try to keep conversations or meetings to 15 or 20 minutes. No matter how busy we are, we can all find 15 or 20 minutes to connect with an acquaintance.

When suggesting a follow-up meeting or chat, consider whether the other party might enjoy getting together at the dog park or taking a morning stroll. Perhaps you could arrange a 15-minute tele-coffee during the week (each party brews a coffee and talks on the telephone) or tele-cocktails on a Friday afternoon (even more fun!). Be creative! Our favorite way to reconnect with friends and colleagues each quarter is with a fabulous evening of *Shoes and Champagne*: I partner with a local shoe boutique and arrange festive champagne and a shopping excursion. A groovy time is always had by all! For the guys, beer and pool might be more appealing.

It is also crucial to devote a few minutes each day to updating online tools such as LinkedIn, Facebook and Twitter. If you've been hesitant to use social networking sites, now is the time to boost your connections by taking advantage of these free and easy opportunities.

To get the most out of a networking site (my favorite is LinkedIn), make sure you take time to learn about its features. When you have a handle on using the site, build your online 'rolodex' by inviting others to be connected to you. Many sites are capable of searching your e-mail accounts for contacts that have established profiles; use this facility to quickly build your connections. Remember to reach out to colleagues from previous employers and business connections, as well as individuals with whom you attended high school, college and graduate school. Do ask others to introduce you to desirable contacts, but first introduce people in your network to one another. I never make a request without making my own introductions first. I often write recommendations for people on LinkedIn, and it is a nice surprise for them in their inbox the next day. Try it out!

## Schedule date nights with loved ones

Of course you don't want to leave your loved ones out of your budgeting: plan to dedicate at least 30 minutes of focused attention each day to the people with whom you share your life. Remind these people that they are special to you by sending a handwritten note or making a quick phone call. If you are pressed for time, create a bulk 'catch-up' e-mail to family and friends letting them know what you have been doing and that you are thinking of them. Above all, don't take your relationships for granted. Live in the moment and spend quality time together.

## Traditional Networking: Getting and Staying Connected

As fun and rewarding as it is to reach out to existing connections, building your career is going to require hitting the pavement for some networking with like-minded but as-of-yet unknown individuals. There are some simple rules to follow in making the most of these opportunities:

**Choose carefully.** Before you commit to a networking event or group, spend time matching events and groups to your professional and personal needs. Determine what you are looking for and ask colleagues to make recommendations.

**Ask questions.** Once you have identified some possibilities, phone the event or group organizer and ask questions to help you decide whether this is a good place to invest your time. For example, what types of people attend this event? Which industries are represented? And so on.

**Become involved.** When you do find a suitable event or group, become a regular and get involved by attending as frequently as possible and volunteering to lend a hand.

**Pay attention.** Strive to be fully present in all conversations when you are meeting new people. Speaking to someone who is clearly distracted or not invested in the moment is unpleasant for both parties. To ensure that you remember each new person's name, repeat it back to him or her when you are making your introductions.

**Don't neglect your business card.** Always carry several business cards, both in and out of business hours. You never know when you will meet someone who may need your services. Make sure that your card is up to date; it should not contain any crossed out or handwritten information.

**Collect cards.** When you have met someone and had a conversation, ask, "May I have your card?" Always ask for the other person's card first. Once you have received it, ask if you may provide your card.

**Ask permission.** If you want to write details on someone's card while you are still with him or her, always ask, "Do you mind if I make a note on the back of your card?" Some individuals invest substantial funds in their cards and asking this question demonstrates your respect.

**Write notes to yourself.** When you have finished a conversation with someone, take a moment to jot down something about the person on the back of his or her card. This will help jog your memory when you contact the person after the event.

**Follow up.** It bears repeating that follow-up is critical. When I schedule a networking event into my calendar, I always book another 30-minute appointment with myself to follow-up with the event organizers and the people I meet.

**Send handwritten cards.** Stand out from the crowd by posting handwritten notes to individuals with whom you made a real connection.

**Send thanks.** Take the time to send thank you notes to event organizers. Let them know that you found the event valuable and include your business card in the envelope.

## Call to Action: Focus Your Energy

When you focus on super-productive connecting, you will find that investing just a little bit of energy each day will pay substantial dividends. I therefore challenge you to allocate just 10 minutes per day to reaching out to contacts; at the end of three months' time, you will have devoted approximately 15 hours to relationship-building without crowding your schedule. Similarly, a mere 15 minutes per day spent on electronic networking will net you 22 hours of connecting in three months' time. Once you get into the habit of focusing on connecting, you will truly be on your way to super-productivity. Now get out there and get connected!

## Know your Impact

Folding Time is achieving twice as much in half the time. The intersection of leverage and engagement in the Folding Time model is impact. So do you ever ask yourself the question … why were you put on this planet?

A deep question I know … and it has everything to do with how you will choose to Fold Time. When you know the purpose of your life, and you keep that front and center in your thoughts and conversations, you will be more likely to spend your energy on the things that make the biggest impact. Do you know your impact?

How do you impact people around you?

What do people enjoy most about being around you?

Who do you impact?

You can have more impact on people you love and care deeply for, and you can also have impact on people who only meet you for a brief moment – every day you can choose to have more impact in the lives of those you touch. To have more impact requires you to make the most of every minute, every opportunity, every interaction. Never underestimate the power of a smile, a genuine thank you, an affectionate touch, a text of encouragement, an email reminding someone you care, giving bunch of flowers for no reason, sending a card, ordering a book for someone – it's the little things that can have a massive impact on someone.

## action plan

Identify someone you admire that has high energy and leverages everything they do.

Write their name here: _____

Make an appointment to interview them for 15 minutes by phone.
**Ask them, "How do you use leverage in your personal and professional life?"**

Write their responses here: _____

_____

_____

_____

_____

_____

Now what will you do differently as a result of reading this chapter? _____

_____

_____

_____

_____

- **Organize and systemize.**
- **Systems create freedom and save you time.**
- **Create day files.**
- **Get your house in order.**
- **Use a visual recognition system.**
- **Invest 15 minutes a day for strategy.**
- **40 minutes will make your day.**
- **Plan tomorrow today.**
- **Conquer email – reduce overwhelm.**
- **Diligently delegate.**
- **Instead of busy; choose right.**
- **Take action.**
- **Be your best in the world.**
- **Devote daily decisions.**
- **Sequence information.**
- **Control technology platforms.**
- **Systemize persistence.**
- **Become a productive road warrior.**
- **Create safe travel systems.**

"Once you have mastered time, you will understand how true it is that most people overestimate what they can accomplish in a year - and underestimate what they achieve in a decade."

- Tony Robbins

## Systems create freedom

Productivity is about deletion not addition: the most productive people I know do less not more.

## Increase productivity at your firm

If you are in a role where you operate a billable hour model, like so many of our professional services firms, implement these strategies to increase the productivity at work.

**Employ professional administrative staff** to reduce the opportunity costs (lost billable time) of anyone involved in management. You might be thinking it is easier and quicker to do it yourself, but this is short-term thinking. Don't waste precious billable hours doing things you are not good at – give it to an admin specialist!

**Stop management from hoarding work and practice delegation** – Choose the highest impact projects or cases to focus your attention on and delegate the rest – simple!

**Provide the high-income earners with tools** to track and report their billable hours. You have heard of the Pareto Principle (or the 80/20 rule); that 80% of your results come from 20% of your efforts. Focus on your top 20% income earners.

**Set individual targets** for income earners and track diligently – people are motivated by success; set big goals and measure them with big rewards.

**Increase training for young associates** to shorten their learning curve and improve productivity sooner – never underestimate the investment training will make in your firm.

When you implement these strategies you will see the productivity of the firm increase and your billable hours will increase also.

## Organize and systemize:
## Systems create freedom - clutter causes captivity

According to the *Wall Street Journal* the average US executive wastes six weeks per year searching for missing information on messy desks – that is nearly an hour a day! It is estimated that this is costing employers $4,000 - $8,125 per employee each year– yikes!

To increase your productivity at work (and home) you need to organize and systemize.

It's not about shuffling papers, making bigger piles or doing the occasional 'spring clean.' Getting organized is very leveraged – clean once, use often!

Take a quick sneak peek at your desk right now: what signals does it send to your co-workers? Do you look organized, professional … in control? OR… do you look like a hot mess? Your workspace is an unconscious message to your team about how organized and systemized you are on a daily basis.

To get additional ideas on this topic we interviewed to our professional organizer Laurie Palau from simply b organized for great advice.

**Make use of vertical wall space** – Hanging in-boxes for important folders clears up valuable desk space allowing you to work in a clean and undistracted workspace.

**Separate items that come across your desk into two piles: one for action and one for reference** For example, if there is a report you need to work on, place it in your **action** file; however, if it's a report you need to keep because you need to refer to it later it belongs in the **reference** file.

**Store papers vertically** as opposed to as a pile on your desk.  This allows for easy referencing and reduces the chances of something important being misplaced.

**Create an electronic filing system thus** eliminating unnecessary clutter on your desk. Added bonus, it takes a fraction of the time to locate electronic documents as opposed to sorting through piles of papers.

**Quick 15 minute clean**: Set your alarm … ready, set, go - in 15 minutes create a system for incoming paper. Consider introducing step file holders for visual recognition, remove all unnecessary stationery from your desk top and throw away all trash.  Voilà … it only takes 15 minutes to create a system and will save you hours each day!

**Eliminate the in-tray** – Remove your in-tray from your desk or get rid of it all together if you can.   Keep it out of sight so the contents don't distract you and so that people don't drop new items into it without you noticing.

Having an overflowing in-tray in front of you can make you feel guilty and tempt you to get distracted from the task at hand.  Educate your colleagues to leave documents for you on your desk where you can see it, and either action or file them as they arrive rather than having them get lost in your ever growing in-tray.

**Create day files** – On our desk we have manila folders each marked Monday through Friday. We have a different color for each day, and they are placed in a step file. This simple system allows us to place papers required for each day (i.e., meeting notes, agendas, items awaiting action), and each day we simply open that file, remove and action the items in it. It is an easy analogue tracking system.

Here are some additional statistics to **scare you into getting organized**:

◀ One in 11 American households rents self-storage space, spending an average of $1,000 per year in rent. Did you know the self-storage industry is a $154 billion dollar per year industry? Crazy!

◀ The US Department of Energy reports that 25% of people with two-car garages have so much stuff there isn't room to park their cars!

◀ 30% of people have lost an important document due to a messy desk.

◀ 47% of people state that disorganization commonly leads to lost time.

◀ 16% say that disorganization leads to meeting tardiness.

◀ 14% say that a messy desk leads to a missed deadline.

◀ People spend six minutes on average each day looking for their keys!

Getting organized is about creating small systems that will allow you to have massive impact. What is one system you could create today that would help you feel more organized, save you time … and potentially save you money?

## Systemization and templates save you time.

**Create templates** – If you find yourself creating proposals, checklists and outlines, the best thing to do is to create a template that you can customize for each request. Saves time and energy. Create once, use often.

**Use a visual recognition system** – Use color-coding to further systemize your files and enable you to identify different types of files at a glance. Choose a range of colored manila folders and allocate a different color to use for different file types; for example, yellow for client files, pink for personal files and so on. Make a reference list of what each color represents so you are familiar with your system.

**Create a media pack** – If you are someone in your industry regularly featured on media, on TV, in the paper or within your community, you will benefit from a media pack. It contains your bio, headshot, brief resume, interesting things about you and possibly even a few questions about your area of expertise the media can use. This media kit is helpful if an opportunity arises and you need to respond quickly. It can also be helpful if you are talking with a perspective client and they want an overview about you – quick and easy to send.

**Create an operations manual** – If you run your own practice, create an operations manual for you and your team. We encourage people who are running a practice to create an operations manual early; as the busier and more profitable you get the less time you have to focus on creating systems. It's never too early to start creating an operations manual.

**Create checklists** – If you travel an enormous amount for your clients across the globe, we recommend using checklists. These simple tools ensure we never forget important items, and we remember to replace them when we return.  You could create standard checklists for grocery shopping, travel, kids sports seasons, birthdays and so many other occasions. Once created, you can use them over and over again. Time invested now saves you time later.  There are great apps available to use frequently.

In our mentoring program we have checklists for the entire process, including paperwork to be completed, outlines for sessions, binder requirements, recommended reading and resources, action plans, follow-up activities and pre-call preparation forms.  These help our office team as well as our mentees to be super prepared for each session to maximize every minute together.

## Work and home systems

**Get your house in order –** You will feel more in control of your life when your home is a retreat rather than an obstacle course or constant reminder of things that need doing.  Spend time spring-cleaning – remove clutter, tidy areas that are distracting to you, create storage solutions and eliminate the mess! It might take you weeks … but the results are worth it. Once your house is in order commit to keeping it that way. If you feel too busy to do it yourself – **hire a professional**.

**Handle mail** – It is amazing to me in such a digital era the volume of paper that still enters our home through the postal system.  Here are a few ways to manage your post:

**Place a 'No Junk Mail' sticker on your mailbox** – This will help the postal service understand you don't wish to receive excessive junk mail.

**Open over the trash** – We open our mail over the trash and immediately recycle paper, shred documents with our address or personal details and file items for actioning.

**Unsubscribe** – Create a letter template to forward to businesses that send junk mail or solicitation requests. Return their mailing piece to them with the request. If you can unsubscribe online, do so; however, this small time investment is well worth the effort both because of time and environmental impact. I HATE junk mail and am on a personal mission to get removed from any list possible.

**Open once a week** – One of our clients only checks her home mailbox on Saturday. Her postal carrier understands she won't be checking it and ensures it all fits in the week. This is very productive. We check our PO Box once a week, as we don't run an urgent business. Can you check it weekly?

## Get Visual Recognition Systems

**Implement your visual recognition systems -** Use color-coding to simplify your life. Growing up in Australia and learning to drive in Australia, I noticed that people obey traffic lights. I have definitely run my share of yellow lights; however, Aussies don't run red lights. Possibly one of the main reasons is because most traffic lights have red light cameras installed, so the moment you run the light, your photo is taken and they kindly send you a fine for your efforts. When moving to the US I was astounded how many people ran red lights (at major intersections) and have totally adjusted my driving style because of this. No, I don't run the lights, but I am more tentative pulling out at a green light if my car is first at the stop line. We grow up understanding the power of the colors of traffic lights.

We can color code many aspects of our life to increase our productivity.

**File management -** In our office we color code files to represent speeches, projects and personal files so at a glance we can see the upcoming speaking engagements and outstanding projects and personal projects.

**Client management** - Maria Novey is a virtual assistant who works for many clients around the USA, and she assigns a color to each client. Of course the color she uses for us is pink! That means the binders, manila folders, plastic sleeves, printing paper, post it notes and envelopes she uses related to the support she provides is always pink. This effective system helps her identify any projects for any client based on color.

**Clothing management** – You can sort your wardrobe by style and color (that sounds a little anal); however, it saves you time and getting ready in the morning. My shoe wardrobe is sorted by color, does that surprise you?

# Work Systems
## 40 minutes of strategy per day

How you spend the first 30 minutes and the last 10 minutes of your day will affect your productivity and achievements – everyday.

When living on Sydney Harbor I would stare out the floor to ceiling glass doors from our gorgeous corner apartment that looked at the harbor bridge (gosh, I miss that view). In the early morning hours I would watch huge container ships make their way into the harbor. What was most fascinating about this picture were the tiny little tug boats that controlled these mammoth ships.

Tug boats are primarily used to tug or pull vessels that cannot move by themselves like disabled ships, oil platforms and barges, or those that should not move – like a big or loaded ship in a narrow canal or a crowded harbor. Did you know that in addition to these, tug boats are also used as ice breakers or salvage boats, and they are built with firefighting guns and monitors? They assist in the firefighting duties especially at harbors and, when required, at sea.

Their guidance, even though they are small, has a massive impact. We need to approach our day by investing a small amount of time for a massive impact.

Most people launch into the day without a second thought; we arrive at the office, unbundle our bags, grab a coffee and start responding to telephones, emails and colleagues – often all at the same time. It's hardly surprising that most people feel like their days are out of control as they fly from one task to the next, and when there is a lull in the excitement – they wonder what to do. It's an exhausting, unsatisfying and unproductive way to work. Even if you are in a position where you need to respond to many demands, investing in the first 30 minutes will pay dividends all day long and just 10 minutes at the end of the day will set you up for the next. If you've ever left the office wondering where the day went or how you could be so busy without achieving anything, try this:

### The first 30 minutes of your day

This is less than 2% of the total amount of time you have a in a day.

**Ignore the ringing in your ears!** Switch your cell phone off or to silent mode, and set your desk phone to voicemail. We have become far too contactable: between telephones, mobiles, text messages, voicemail and email it is possible to spend your entire day responding to other people.

Are you one of those people who cannot bear the thought of not answering a ringing phone? The phone is a tool for your convenience – use and respond to it when it suits you. Try thinking of a ringing phone as question – it's someone asking you if you are available to speak – and it's your choice whether it suits you to speak now or to let the call go through to voicemail and respond later.

You'll be more productive allowing yourself a clear head to focus on what needs to be achieved without breaking your train of thought every time the phone rings – and it's more considerate to your caller. We've all had the experience when someone who is clearly busy, distracted, frustrated or in a rush answers our call – it puts both people in an uncomfortable position. It would have been fairer for them to allow us to leave a message and to respond at a more convenient time. Be sure to develop good practices for calling people back – this means determining the urgency and importance of the call-back and making sure you respond appropriately. Overtime, people will learn that you are not always available, they'll respect the way you manage your time and trust you to get back to them.

**Hang a 'Do Not Disturb' sign.** This phrase could have originated from a Latin phrase "Do not disturb my circles." That is, "Don't upset my calculations!" said by Archimedes to a Roman soldier who, despite having been given orders not to, killed Archimedes at the conquest of Syracuse, Sicily. The soldier was executed for his act.

Have you ever stayed at a Ritz Carlton property? They are forbidden to knock on a door if you have this sign on your door handle.

Have you ever watched people at the customs line at the international airports? As you reenter the country you will see huge lines of very tired, jet lagged individuals who know that they MUST stand behind the yellow line. No one even has to say this, they know not to disturb the customs officer, and they wait their turn before they approach them. The yellow line becomes a do-not-disturb sign.

If you have an actual office with a door, this one is easy, but many workplaces today are open office plan, and it's difficult to alert people to the fact that you don't wish to be interrupted – but there are ways around it.

One of our pharmaceutical clients, who has an open plan office, created a system where each person has an item (in this case, a koosh ball) which when placed on top of their computer means that they are not available – that they are trying to concentrate on something. When the koosh ball comes down, everyone knows they are available again. With the agreement of everyone in the team, this system works particularly well for an open plan environment.

An article in *USA Today* in 2011 stated that more than 50% of US workers waste an hour or more a day on interruptions: 60% come from electronic devices and emails while the other 40% come from traditional sources, such as phone calls or chats with colleagues.

**Use headphones.** When people see you have headphones on they know you are not tuned-in to what's happening around you – you don't even have to be listening to anything if you find that too distracting – just put your headphones on to signal your do-not-disturb request.

Alternatively, if you have the option, complete your first 30-minutes off-site – perhaps at home or at a local café where you can find a quiet, comfortable corner so that when you arrive at the office you are ready to face the challenges and opportunities of the day with a clear plan.

**Book a meeting with yourself.** Block-out the first 30-minutes in your calendar. Treat it as a standing commitment and protect it from being taken by other people's meeting requests. Overtime, people will learn that you are not available until a certain time (which will vary depending on when you schedule your 30-minutes), and they'll work around you.

**Tell everyone.** Whatever system you do use, even if it is physically closing your office door, it's important to let your team know what you're doing and why – so they'll learn to understand and respect your quiet time and work around it. Encourage others to also use the first 30 minutes practice – with the benefit of planning and thinking time everyone's results will improve.

**Prepare for the day ahead.** Use your 30 minutes to review your calendar for the day: block out meeting times, including travel time to-and-from appointments and a lunch break. (Yes, you do need to eat and take a break away from your desk, if only for a few minutes.)

My friend and legendary DJ Mike Walter in his book *Ten Things You Can Do To Have a Better Day* shares the following tip: **avoid screen eating**. What a great term for it! If you are eating in front of your computer, iPad, iPhone or TV you don't get to really enjoy and savor the meal – make a note to avoid this habit today and take a break away from your desk (and technology).

Now look at how much time is left to 'do work' and schedule tasks realistically – remember that on average, things take two-to-three times longer than we expect them to. **Most people's to-do lists end up being impossibly long; we're not likely to get through them in a month, let alone by the end of the day, so it's important to prioritize your daily tasks**.

**Ask yourself:** "If I could only accomplish three things on my list today, which would deliver the best results?" This is a question that thought leader Stacey Hanke asks herself daily – these are your top priorities and where you need to focus your efforts. It can also be beneficial to write these three priorities on a post-it note to keep a visual reminder where to focus today.

Your day may not end up looking as chaotic and jam-packed as you're used to, but you will find you achieve more and are more in-control of your time – and the bonus is, you'll feel better and produce a better quality of work.

## Plan tomorrow today

Schedule your day – invest 10 minutes at the end of the day to schedule your next day activities, remember to block out time to exercise and time to eat.

**Quitting time.** Schedule time at the end of your day; just like for your first 15 to 30 minutes, you need to block-out the last 10 minutes of your day to make time for your end-of-day routine.

**Look ahead**. Start your to-do list for the next day. The best time to do this is at the end of the day when your focus is still on the job – it's far more difficult to do in the morning when you're wondering where you left off the day before.

**Carry over incomplete tasks** from your current day's list and add new priorities. It helps to clear your head and put it to paper, and you'll be amazed at how much more effective you can be when your brain power is being put to problem-solving rather than trying to remember everything you need to do! It helps, too, to give you a clearer picture of what needs to be achieved and what you can delegate. There's enormous satisfaction in being able to check-off completed items and review your achievements at the end of the day!

**What's in store?** Check your calendar and commitments for the following day and be aware of what's coming up, where you need to be and what preparation, tasks and projects you need to focus on.

**Leave it clean**. Clear and tidy your desk, throw trash away, sort leftover mail and papers and put your files away; apart from being good housekeeping, it is good for office security to have valuable company information filed away in locked cabinets or drawers. By clearing your workspace you also signal the end of the day and clear your mind. This is important regardless of whether you work in a home or office.

**Wash up.** Clean your coffee cup, empty your water bottle, wash any leftover dishes or containers from lunch and start each day afresh.

**Carry your reading**. Put your physical reading file in your briefcase or create a folder on your iPad for reading. If you don't already have one, start a reading file and carry it with you on your way home. You can get through a surprising amount of reading while on public transport to and from work and while waiting in queues.

**Spend time clearing**. Give yourself permission each afternoon to clear your thoughts. Make time to clear your desk and your files. This feeling of 'clear' will allow you to feel lighter and focus more intently the next day. This can be a great exercise before you walk into your home at night to avoid taking work into your home-life. Clear.

**Shut down.** Switch your phone to voicemail, remembering to change your message if you're not going to be in the next day, or if you're going to be in late. Close email, again, remembering to activate your out-of-office message if you're not going to be in the next day, and switch off your computer, screen & printer.

# Electronic Systems
## Conquer your Email: Reduce Overwhelm
Email was originally designed to increase your communication effectiveness. It was a tool to do your job … some days it feels like THE job. Don't let email overwhelm you. By implementing these strategies you can conquer your email – get more done so you can get on with it!

**Conquer in 15 minutes** – Invest 15 dedicated (not multi-tasking) minutes to your email in scheduled times through the day. Focus, read, action, delete! Don't be a slave to your email inbox.

**Turn off bells, whistles and envelopes** - Any kind of reminder or sound – mute it immediately. These constant interruptions distract and decrease your effectiveness.

**Drag and drop** – Did you know that if you are using Microsoft Outlook and you highlight an email in your inbox, you could drag it to create a new task, or a new contact or a new calendar appointment? This simple action will save you an enormous amount of time.

**Use an electronic signature** – use your email program to create an email signature block that will automatically attach to all your outgoing messages. It saves you time and effort and makes it easier for everyone receiving your emails to get in contact with you. Always include full contact information and possibly a sentence or two about your business, offerings or upcoming programs.

**Diligently Use "Out-of-Office"–** If you are unable to respond to emails or you will be out of your office for a long period of time, set up an out-of-office auto-responder for your email. This manages others' expectations about response times.

**Don't copy the world** – Seriously, only send email to relevant people who will action it. If you copy multiple people on an email, list their name within the body of the email and the action required and due date. People appreciate a direct approach.

**Unsubscribe!** Get off the lists of emails you never read or lists you don't want to be on. Many specialized applications and websites are now designed to help you eliminate messages you won't read (there are many for those of you using Gmail or Google apps).

**Think and write in bullet points** – Keep sentences short and to the point. Don't use email to create long paragraphs or criticize performance.

**Always use a greeting** – Take time to greet in email just like you do in person. Systemize this as part of your email signature and that way it is always there!

**Master email functionality**– Invest time in learning email functionality and short cuts to maximize email.

**Set up email rules** – Establish rules for incoming email to help you sort the legitimate messages from spam, jokes and junk. Your email program can help you – get to know the functionality of the system you use daily.

**Use a visual recognition system** - Color code your inbox so at a glance you respond to your inbox quickly to most important first.

**Use your subject line as your email body** – If you can request or write in the subject line, don't add a body – use EOM (end of message).

**Remember screen size has decreased** – People don't all read emails on a computer … mostly it is on smart phones at red lights. (I am sure you don't email and drive … right?) Keep your message short!

**Check email three-four times per day** – Not all day! Significant time is wasted responding to emails throughout the day. Focus energy on checking and responding only three-four times a day: once when you start your day, after lunch then one hour before you leave your office. This will ensure you can handle important communication in a timely manner.

**Delete once actioned** – Don't let emails stay in your inbox; this is not your to-do list. Once actioned, delete. If you need to take action from the email, schedule time to complete the task and then delete it.

**Allocate 15 minutes every Friday** to file actioned emails you want to archive.

**Don't make email more important than people** – If the subject of your communication requires interaction, consider if email is the best format; would a short call or meeting have more impact? This also means that if you have someone in your office or a meeting – pay attention to them.

**Don't return every email** – Don't respond to CC emails. Kim Woodworth, executive at Comcast Spotlight, and I were recently discussing email management and a great system she uses relates to emails that are CC (carbon copied) to her.

- ◀ If the cc'd email is from her boss or positions higher than her boss, she reads it carefully and responds. (If a response is needed from CC participation).
- ◀ If the cc'd email is from her peers she reviews it in bullets and determines if a response is necessary (often not).
- ◀ If the cc'd email is from anyone else she scans the email and doesn't respond.

This is a powerful and effective system for email management.

**Don't get overwhelmed** – Get control of your email inbox today and maximize your productivity.

Have you ever completed a detox? This can be an important jumpstart for your body if you have taken medications, indulged too much in the holiday celebrations or you aren't feeling 100%. Detoxes can be mild or severe depending on the results you want and your willingness to commit to significant changes for a period of time.

Due to advice from a nutritionist, I went cold turkey on sugar – all sugar. Sugar is found in almost everything we eat, and my detox included natural sugars like fruit. The crazy part of this detox from sugar was the side effects I didn't expect. My energy plummeted, and I got the shakes; yes that's right – my hands were shaking. My diet is healthy, I don't eat anything from fast food franchises, I am gluten-free so I avoid nasty white flour and related junk food products … BUT I ate a lot of fruit!

The removal of these items from my diet had such a big effect on my body, I couldn't believe it. Besides weight loss, an interesting side effect was clearer focus.

Sometimes we have to delete things from our everyday in order to increase our effectiveness or jumpstart a new system.

Note: you will be pleased to know I am now allowed to have fruit, but I do limit it more than I used to.

## Diligently delegate

True delegation is taking 80% of your work and doing it, 10% of your work and giving it to someone else and allowing you to do 10% stretch work (maybe you can ask your boss or leadership to share with you something you can learn).

**Delegate 10%** - You must delegate at least 10% of your work to someone else to allow them to grow their skill set and allow you to stretch yourself by learning 10% new skills.

**Pareto works here** – The 80/20 rule definitely works when it is applied to delegation. Remember his theory that 80% of Italy's landmass was controlled by 20% of the population? What is the 20% of activities that truly requires your focus and how much can you delegate to others?

## Be active, not busy

Focus on high return activities instead of busyness. We can fill our days with busy; however, we need to focus on the activities that give us higher results.  One of the CEOs we worked with in our mentoring program was still doing the weekly book keeping for her firm. This sounds crazy; however, she wanted to know every single detail, and it was being done at night and on weekends — not productive. We found her a mobile financial controller she could trust and work with who managed the small details so she could concentrate on the big details. She was busy doing data entry and not actively pursuing the company's financial goals. Focus on high return activities first.

Hummingbirds are fascinating to me. They drink nectar, a sweet liquid inside certain flowers. Like bees, they are able to assess the amount of sugar in the nectar they eat; they reject flower types that produce nectar that is less than 10% sugar and prefer those whose sugar content is stronger.  They focus their attention on the flowers that are most beneficial for them.

They are tiny creatures and do not spend all day flying because the energy cost would be prohibitive; the majority of their activity consists simply of sitting or perching.  Hummingbirds feed in many small meals, consuming many small invertebrates and up to 12 times their own body weight in nectar each day. They spend an average of 10–15% of their time feeding and 75–80% sitting and digesting.

They have it right! They are active and focused on the activities that are most beneficial for their survival – how can we be more like hummingbirds?

### Instead of busy – choose right

Sometimes we create crazy long to-do lists, however maybe the wrong things are making it on our list. Take a moment to review your to-do list. Does every item on that list have to be done? Does it have to be done by you? Is there someone who can help you? Is there someone better equipped to complete that? What would happen if you didn't do it? Instead of being constantly busy we need to choose the right items to for our time, attention and energy.

**Use one to-do list –** Regardless of paper or electronic, create one list that covers your personal and business activities – it makes it easier to locate and easier to cross items off once completed.

## Systems at Home

Some of our clients share that they are super organized at work (because they have to be) but don't have similar systems at home. Why is this?

Creating a productive space at home is essential for your sanity. You don't want to spend weekends cleaning, organizing or being overwhelmed. A few simple ideas can help your home flow smoothly.

### Sunday sanity savers

**Soup Sundays –** Allocate time on a Sunday to cook a few freezer friendly meals. I like to make soups in the winter and pop them in the freezer or share them with neighbors. Soup is a healthy and quick lunch option. Doesn't take much time and is rewarding, too.

**Outline outfits –** Review your weekly schedule and allocate a small space in your wardrobe to place all the outfits you will need for the week. Include the clothing, shoes and accessories. Fabulous stylist Megan Kristel, owner of Kristel Closets, has a small whiteboard installed in their clients' wardrobes so they can write each day and the outfit they need – love that!

**Group errands together** – If you are still doing your own errands (and haven't sweet talked one of your kids or the local neighbor in it) group them all together. Make a list in the sequence you want to complete them, and fill your car with everything you need so you head out once and achieve an enormous amount. If you have returns, postage, dry cleaning, groceries to collect – save it all up and do it at the same time.

**Don't put it down, put it away** – My Aunty Carol used to say this when I was little, "Create a habit to avoid placing items where they don't belong - spend an extra moment putting things away." This is an essential skill to teach every member of the family so you don't waste time cleaning up or tidying after everyone else. This new habit saves time.

When you are cooking consider putting ingredients away as you are finished with them, loading the dishwasher as you go and putting things back in cabinets before you sit down to eat. When you take off an outfit, determine if it goes in the laundry hamper, dry cleaner or back in your wardrobe.

**Tip**: Hang a bag inside your wardrobe for dry cleaning items and have them picked up weekly.

**Separate cutlery** – When you are loading the dishwasher, put all like items together. You can teach others in your home to do the same thing and then unpacking is quicker.

**Do laundry twice a week** – Instead of saving it all up and dreading it on a weekend, do a load or two during the week so that you feel more accomplished and organized.  Fold items as they come out of the dryer and put away loads regularly.

**Buy pre-made or prewashed** – During your grocery trips seek out salad items that are pre-washed to make it quicker at night when you are preparing dinner. In a survey published in the April 2010 *Real Simple Magazine,* 31% of people shared that they felt guilty splurging on prewashed lettuce – funny – don't feel guilty – just do it!

## Take Action

Luck is for wimps; action is for heroes. "Luck may or may not be on your side BUT action is 100% within your control," says Sally Hogshead in *Radical Careering*.

Sally is so right! As the author of *Fascinate,* she is a brilliant speaker and this quote got me thinking … we need to spend less energy talking about what COULD or SHOULD be done … and just get on with it! Productivity is about all the small choices we make on a daily basis.

It's not about luck – it's about taking action.

## Get uncomfortable

If you find yourself in a comfort zone at work or in your personal life it is time to take action to change it up; increase activity, focus on health or do something that takes you outside your comfort zone. I hired a personal trainer (holy guacamole, Batman … boy is that uncomfortable) – before leaving the studio my body is uncomfortable but I know that the discomfort means progress. Where do you need to get uncomfortable?

## Start small win big

Focus attention on the small daily decisions that are affecting your action. Concentrate on completing activities within 15 minute increments, i.e., answer email, go for a quick walk, call a client to thank them for their business or have a face to face conversation with someone you care about. Your small daily decisions will help you achieve massive results!  What small decisions could you make daily that would give you massive returns?

## Don't talk ... just do it

Nike's ad agency Weiden & Kennedy and a group of their employees were onto something in 1988 when they created this simple but memorable slogan, "Just do it." We need to take this to heart – less talk, more action. If you want to increase your productivity just do it. If you want to reduce your email, stop sending so many. If you want to get healthy, go for a walk!

Productivity is not about talking, it is about taking action. Spend less energy talking about what should be done and focus on getting it done. What can you **just start** this week to get you closer to your goals?

When people tell me I am "so lucky," I smile. I know it is not luck that achieves goals, it is action. All the heroes I admire (especially Wonder Woman) took action. What action can you take today?

## Be Your Best in the World – Don't Quit

In *The Dip*, Seth Godin says, "Quit or be exceptional. Average is for losers." He adds that we need to quit the wrong stuff and stick to the right stuff, and have the guts to do one or the other.

In this book, Godin shares that there are seven reasons people fail: they run out of time, money, get scared, aren't serious, lose interest, focus on short term instead of long term and pick the wrong thing – yes, that all makes sense, and we can relate to many of those reasons.

Success is a choice; a choice to work through when things become hard, keep going when it is easy to become distracted and when you decide NOT to quit you are on your way to excelling at what you choose to do.

Malcolm Gladwell in his book *Outliers* states that individuals need 10,000 hours to become good at something. Many of the case studies, he shares, showcase people willing to stick at something, to not quit until they became the best in the world.

I have heard it said, "If it scares you it might be a good thing to do." Some projects (or people) feel overwhelming and scary when we begin; however, after investing time and attention with the project or person we realize we can do this.

Execution is about systemizing what you can and having the courage to keep going even when times feel tough and you want to give up.

## Devote Daily Decisions
Assign activities to particular days to increase execution.

While in high school (which was a really, really long time ago) we had a timetable. We had certain classes (or periods as they were called in Australia) on certain days. This simple system worked effectively to cover the entire curriculum and also created a variety to keep students engaged. (Well, I assume that was the idea.) Wednesday afternoons we had physical education (PE). This was not my favorite subject. Not being born with an athletic physique I was happy to trade this time to volunteer with the students who had learning difficulties. Spending several hours on Wednesdays with them reading, testing, and spelling was so rewarding – it was great (much better than running around unglamorously in the Australian heat). I always associated Wednesdays with great memories.

While working with a District Sales Manager at a media company, we found his demanding role involved giving his time to his team and clients. This frustrated him because he wasn't able to achieve his own work and complete projects he wanted to finish. He felt trapped between all the requests coming from senior leadership above him and all the daily tactical requests from his team. In desperation, he called and we developed a day system. We allocated important strategic projects (and thinking time) to certain days in the week based on the workflow and demands of a regular week.

After implementing this for only three weeks, he saw a huge increase in his productivity and a huge decrease in his stress levels.

What activities can you allocate to certain days?

## Sequence Information: Reduce overwhelm and increase impact

While speaking for one of our oil & gas clients, we met with one of the leaders before the live webcast discussing how she was an incredibly valuable resource within her company. Her extensive experience as an administrative professional meant she was the go-to-gal for a variety of applications, processes and especially information.

After interviewing her we discovered her secret … it was her ability to sequence information.

She is regularly bombarded with constant requests for her time and attention, and there is always someone wanting her to do something, be somewhere or have something completed.

Does this sound like you?

If you want to reduce overwhelm and increase your impact, try these strategies to sequence how you respond to information daily.

**Know your 20%** - What are the activities in your day that allow you to achieve 80% of your results? Remember Pareto's principle (80/20 rule) — it is especially applicable to how we choose to invest our time daily. Focus on your 20% of activities and information that helps achieve your goals.

**Know your agenda** – Just like every meeting needs an agenda to be productive, every person needs an agenda each day. What are the goals and objectives for your day? When you are clear about your agenda you choose which activities and requests to respond to first.

**Know your methodology** – Let the people in your life know the best way to communicate with you. Are you an email girl (or guy)? Do you prefer phone calls, or chatting face to face? Once others know your preferred style they can communicate with you in this way. Always ask people you work with, "What is the best way to communicate with you? And make a note of their preference.

Sequencing is knowing the order in which things happen – you get to choose daily how you manage information and requests.

According to BBC News, web browsing has shortened our attention span to nine seconds – less than a goldfish! That's scary.

What can you do today to reduce overwhelm by sequencing information?

## Control Technology Platforms

We all agree that technology has changed the pace at which we work. We can now do things quicker, easier and sometimes cheaper. It has also provided us with more choices; more demands on our time and sometimes instead of increasing our productivity… it kills our productivity.

Choose today to embrace tools that support you, learn applications that make your job easier and eliminate the distractions that rob you of your time.

**Know your needs -** Research the best tools to achieve your goals. Do you need a laptop because you travel, a smart phone or tablet to avoid carrying a laptop, or a desktop because you need a large screen for design? Understand which tools are going to be most beneficial for you.

**Know the applications -** When you own or purchase technology invest the time to learn the applications provided (especially short cuts for programs and quick reference guides) - leverage the functionality of each application.

**Use DropBox** – We love this application for sharing files in the cloud that you and your team can access from anywhere, with any tools! Find a cloud system you enjoy and leverage it.

**Invest in maintenance -** Allocate time monthly to maintaining technology. Schedule time to defrag your computer, install new software, delete unused applications, remove large files and back-up data. Scheduling time each month will ensure your technology runs at an optimum level regularly. Consider setting up automatic backups of your computer systems.

**Outsource maintenance** – If all this technology maintenance isn't your thing, get help – delegate. Find a local business or college student that can assist you with this activity monthly.

**Back up weekly!** – Why is it we wait until something goes wrong before we think about backing up our computers and technology? Schedule weekly back-ups to ensure you always have the latest information available. This became even more important to me when I had a laptop stolen; it sure does make you wish you had backed up more often!

**Check email four times per day** – Seriously, some people are addicted to their email and that isn't productive! **Unless you are a brain surgeon or deliver babies**

**… or maybe cure cancer** – you don't need to be checking email every few minutes. Allocate time throughout the day to check it (and delete it), but don't be on email all day!

**Use Out-of-Office messages** – Every email system has the ability to advise people that you are away. If you leave for long meetings, go on vacation or just want to focus on a project for a few hours, use out-of-office to manage others' expectations.

**Update voicemail weekly** – Allow callers to know where you are going to be and how they can best reach you. Share alternative connection strategies like cell phones, email or your assistant's number. (If you are lucky enough to have an assistant!)

**Use the on/off buttons on everything** – Conserve electricity and get into the habit of turning off items not in use. This can also be a great tip if you work from home and get tempted to check your laptop at all hours … turn it off!

**Video meetings** – There are valuable video tools, like Google+ and Skype, which allow you to have conversation with multiple people, and if you use video in your meeting, partners won't be multi-tasking! It avoids the need to travel to and from meetings, and you can do it from the comfort from your office or home.

**Consider alternative meetings methods** – One is Skype; another is my favorite tele-coffees (you make a coffee, and I make a coffee, and we chat on the telephone) — it takes no more than 15 minutes! I do tele-cocktails on Fridays – love those!

**Shorten meetings** – stop making meetings 30 or 60 minutes in length, reduce meetings to 20 or 40 minutes instead. When you give people time back you will look like a rock star! Everyone compresses everything they need into the time allocated (or worse … people will expand conversations into the time allocated) – save time, shorten meetings.

**Limit time to 15 minutes!** Stop wasting time clicking on one link after another – focus, set your target for the information you need to find and go find it. It is amazing how time disappears when we start to play online!

Technology is a tool designed to help you do your job, increase productivity and increase communications … it is not supposed to kill your productivity. Applying these strategies will ensure that when you use the right tools, set your time limits and know your systems, you will definitely increase your productivity!

## Systemize Persistence

Create a consistent follow-up system to increase your connection and expand opportunities.

**Create a follow-up checklist –** This could be used for client meetings, after networking meetings or after presentations. Create once, use often.

**Use LinkedIn –** After someone has used your products or services, request a recommendation from them on LinkedIn to share with other potential clients.

**Use electronic task management –** If you enjoy Outlook, use the task function; if you are a Mac user find an app you enjoy that provides electronic reminders of due tasks, i.e., Things or Google Apps Do.

## Outsource Your Life - Systems at Home

**Invest in capacity** – Choose to increase your productivity by teaching others, delegating and helping build their skill sets. You'll give others the satisfaction of learning something new, reward them with more responsibility, free up your own headspace to focus on other important things and empower everyone to achieve more.

Henry David Thoreau said, "A man is rich in proportion to the number of things he can afford to let alone."

One summer, my husband bought us tickets to see a Russian Symphony at the gorgeous location of the Mann Center in Philadelphia. It was such a special night as everyone was dressed up and sat back to revel in the magic of the music that was created for us. I couldn't take my eyes off the conductor – his flair, precision, and his trust in the musicians. They all watched him carefully, obeying his every command. Each short or long hand gesture meant something to those observing him. It was truly fascinating. The conductor didn't need to know how to play every instrument; however, he did need to direct the orchestra, delegate the playing of each instrument to the talented individuals and as result, everyone was empowered to play their finest music.

**Shop online** – Remove time wasted in stores for items you don't need to touch and feel and have them delivered. The Internet has endless options for ordering groceries, supplies and even fresh lobster!

**Be the conductor** – Recruit those around you to help execute what needs to be done. Trust their skills and abilities and outsource your life where you can.

**Use home delivery** – Instead of schlepping from one store to the next, use delivery services.

**Use a cleaning service** – I believe if you are earning more than $30K per year and you are still cleaning your house, that's just stupid! Unless you LOVE to clean (I am not one of those people) then hire someone to help you.

**Use a lawn service** – If you spend substantial time on your weekends doing lawn maintenance, consider using a service to give you time back.

**Hire a taxi or limo** – Instead of driving to the airport, can you use a car service to allow you to get work done on the way to the airport? Where we live sometimes I wish I had a helicopter service to avoid traffic!

**Use inexpensive services online** – There are many websites dedicated to inexpensive completion of tasks, such as fiverr.com where you can get many things done for only $5.

## Travel Systems: Become a Productive Road Warrior

You have seen them, they all look alike, the regular road warrior with their determined expression, wrinkle proof suit and pulling a beaten up carry-on bag. Whether you travel a little or a lot with your business there are many ways you can boost your personal productivity when you travel. These before, during and after strategies will help you maximize your time, limit your stress and overall increase your travel productivity.

## Before You Travel

**Buy the tools** – You wouldn't build a house without the right tools, and travel is no different. To be a productive traveler you want to ensure you have a variety of tools to assist the comfort and productivity of your trip. Tools to consider purchasing are quality luggage, iPod, noise cancelling earphones and your smartphone.

**20-22 inch Carry-On expandable luggage** – We love Briggs and Riley, it is durable, lightweight, expandable, self-healing and well made. These are allowed in the US and other countries as carry-on baggage. When you are buying luggage look for features such as pull along, strong wheels, stability foot on the bottom (in case it gets too heavy), external zippers (to hold travel documentation and the Ziploc toiletry bag), and also make sure the pop up handle is a one pull action.

**iPod** – This is not a luxury; this is a requirement for any travel. Create a selection of play lists, including one with very relaxing music so that when it is time to sleep, you can turn to this group. It is also great to have a groovy list for working out.

**Noise cancelling earphones** – These might be a luxury, but I wouldn't travel anywhere without them. My husband previously flew many long international flights, and he turned me onto this great invention. The small Sony ear bud type works well, and take them wherever you go

**Briefcase** – A soft tote briefcase that allows you to include personal and work related items. When looking for a brief case, also make sure it has the feature to slide over your carry-on luggage (many have a soft strap or a zippered section to allow you to do this). Our favorite is the Brookline Tote by Lo & Sons.

**Consider clothing** – When you are regularly on the road we suggest a few strategies to help make your life easier for both packing and arriving looking put together.

**Travel Outfit** – Create your own travel outfit; yes, it can be the same every time. A pair of black pants, a black top (have a short sleeved one for summer and a long sleeved one for cooler months) and a pair of black patent leather flat slip on shoes – flats or stilettos work. Wear the same jewelry when you arrive at the security line you don't have to remove anything (except shoes) – that is why pantyhose (or socks) are good when you have to take off your shoes. The fabric of this outfit shouldn't crease and should be comfortable (which makes a huge different on those long flights).

**Airport shoes** – Think about the quality and make of the shoes you wear to the airport. We suggest slip-ons of some description so you are not awkwardly trying to tie up laces or straps. Also, ensure they are comfortable and well made, as you often have to walk long distances between gates or to the parking area.

**Carry a pashmina** – For the ladies, we recommend you invest in a dark colored pashmina that has many uses. On the plane it is a great blanket (and many airlines in the US don't supply pillows and blankets). When I rent a car it becomes a booster seat for me. When I have to sit on an airport floor (yes, I have done that living in the US) it is great to place on the floor … oh and yes, you can wear it if you need to keep warm.

**Jewelry** – Wear the same jewelry when you travel and walk through the screening area without having to remove it. It simplifies the process and speeds up the line.

**Belts** – If possible, don't wear an outfit that requires a belt; it is one more item of clothing you have to remove at the airport security line.

**Productive Packing** – There are many opinions on what to pack, and we find the most productive way for me is having a series of pre-packed bags. This includes luggage, carry-on plane survival kit, brief case, make-up and toiletry bags.

**Pre-packed luggage** contents includes:
- Ziploc toiletry bag
- Underwear
- First aid items (band aids, safety pins and headache tablets)
- Make up bag
- Gym gear
- Clothes brush
- Book of interest
- Chargers for all your electronics
- Stamped stationery (note cards and envelopes)

**Carry-on plane** survival kit contents include:
- iPod
- Noise cancelling earphones
- Spare battery for noise cancelling earphones
- Lip balm
- Eye mask (for long flights)
- Pen
- Eye drops
- Travel size toothbrush and toothpaste
- Breath mints

**Make-up kit** – Ladies, if you travel regularly we suggest you buy a full set of make-up, make-up brushes and tools, and keep in a separate make-up bag so that you never have to go looking for something, and you never forget something on your trips.

**Ziploc Toiletry Bag** contents include travel sized:
- Decanted shower gel
- Skin care
- Hair care
- Travel sized perfume or aftershave (most brands now supply a smaller size compliant with airline safety standards)
- Toothpaste

Many department stores and pharmacies carry a range of **travel-sized products**. Sephora has merchandising near the payment counter, which includes 50+ choices of regular products in travel sized convenient containers.

**Plastic helps** – My friend Camille Valvo was an airline goddess for many years and provided this great tip: using the plastic you receive from your dry cleaners to wrap around your clothes helps avoid creases.

**Duplicate copies** – To be more productive (and for a few extra dollars), consider investing in duplicates of everything you travel with. If you are a regular traveler, having a pre-packed bag will allow you to leave with minimum notice and save time and stress before any trip. On your list of items to buy you could include:

- ◀ Toiletries available in travel size
- ◀ Brushes – make-up brushes, hair brushes or combs
- ◀ Cell phone charger
- ◀ Laptop power pack
- ◀ Make-up
- ◀ Stamps and stationery
- ◀ Spare items, i.e., pantyhose, clothing brush.
- ◀ Gym clothes and shoes

**Choose your seat** – We like to sit in an aisle seat to get in and out while avoiding feeling cramped by others. For longer flights (especially the red eye), some people enjoy the window seat so they can lean against the window to sleep. Choose your seat wisely. If you have an option of an exit row choose this seat as it gives you more legroom. You may like to check out www.seatguru.com – it is a great website to see exactly what your seat will be on most major airlines.

**Pre-print or download your boarding pass** – Go online 24 hours before you fly and select your seat; print your boarding pass or send it to your smartphone. This will save you time in the long lines at the airport check in and also help you find the seat you want.

**Join airline clubs** – If you fly frequently to the same cities, join the airline programs of those major airlines so you can also gather frequent flyer miles for all your travels. You may be able to use them for a fun trip with those you care for later on.

**Join airline lounges** – If you fly with the same carrier regularly, invest in a membership for that lounge so you have a quiet place to snack, get changed or to catch-up on reading. I noticed in Australia that this was a great use of money and well worth it; however, in the US the gates and lounges are so spread out, and there are so many options to travel with different airlines, that this hasn't been a worthwhile investment for me here, but if you fly the same airline every time it might be worth it for you.

**Get a Platinum Amex** – This provides entrance to many airline lounges.

**Create a one-page itinerary** – Create a one-page template that includes your confirmation codes and all flight details, hotel and rental car information. Also include on this template all your frequent flyer clubs and associations so that if you arrive and they haven't included this in your booking you can quickly get credit for your travel.

**Create your out of office system** to automatically advise others and manage their expectations.

## During Your Travel

**Allow extra 30 minutes** – Add at least 30 minutes onto any amount of time you think it will take you to get to the airport or park. This additional time will save you stress if you are stuck in traffic, can't find a parking space or the security line is longer than you expected. If you have pre-packed a book or magazine you can use that 30 minutes to read or to connect with a friend or client.

**Know the parking garage** – If you regularly travel on the same airline, know the shuttle system or design of the car park so you can get in and out quickly. Park on the same level each time (we always park on level 3).

**Take your ticket** – When receiving a parking receipt/ticket on your arrival, place it in the same compartment of your bag or briefcase so you know where to find it upon return.

**Write the parking space on your ticket** – In the US, the parking garages are so big we write the color and space on our parking receipt so that when arriving back after a few days away (often late at night), we can quickly find the car and not waste time wandering around the parking garage. There are also great apps you can use to help you find your car and parking spot.

**Ground transport notice** – When you enter an airport, notice where the taxis, rental car shuttles or parking garages are. This will save you time when you return and allow you to quickly make your way to the next place.

**Regular rental** – Use the same rental company each time you travel; this will also boost your productivity because you will expect a certain standard each time you fly. You might also consider joining their frequent customer program. I like using Enterprise because they are affordable, and also each time you arrive they look so happy to see you. They also pay attention to small details including water bottles in the car and pre-printed local lists of radio stations and areas of interest.

**Play music** – Create different play lists on your iPod; you will enjoy your travel more if you can listen to music and block out the noise around you. This is effective in the airport lounge, at the gate and on the plane. Get the adapters necessary to play in your iPod in rental cars, too.

**Getting through security** – Several tips to help you get through the line faster:
- Enroll in the fast track systems.
- Wear an outfit that doesn't require any removal of items or have metal.
- Place your cell phone and keys into your briefcase or purse before entering the security line.
- Keep your Ziploc bag of toiletries in an outside zippered compartment for quick access.
- Get your laptop out of your briefcase before you reach your place in line.
- Place your laptop, shoes and toiletries in one container on the security screening belt.
- Keep your boarding pass and photo identification in your hands.

**Check-in or carry-on** – We always carry-on our luggage (up to a five day business trip). We have learned to pack well and invested in a minimum number of outfits. There is so much time wasted waiting for luggage. (Not to mention the concern that it may not arrive with you!) Wherever possible, try to carry-on luggage for your business travel.

**Keep a reading file** – As you collect articles, newspapers or journals you want to read, take them with you when you travel.

**Buy bottled water** – Establish your routine: as soon as you get through the security line, head to the nearest store to buy two bottles of water. During the flight it is essential to drink water to keep you hydrated, and two bottles allows you to drink before the plane arrives (this has been helpful when there are large delays) and during the flight.

**Eat healthy** – Airlines don't supply quality food on board. Find healthy solutions within the airport to satisfy your hunger. You may also like to buy something to eat on board for longer flights so you are snacking on healthy items. You could travel with a bag of almonds and pecans, dried fruit or granola bars so you always have a yummy (and healthy) snack available. As you are flying from the same airport each week become familiar with the food offerings inside the terminal so you can quickly find something you enjoy eating.

**Pack snacks** – With so many people having food allergies now, it is essential you know what you are putting in your body. Travel constantly with snacks. Over the years, we've learned that the following items travel well and make it through security: bananas, almonds, protein powder for shakes, protein bars, Lara Bars, corn chips and blueberries in a container.

**Hotel routine** – No matter what time you arrive at your hotel, have the same routine. Open your suitcase, remove your outfit and hang it. If it has gathered small creases during travel, take it into the bathroom, hang it up and turn on the hot shower to create a steam room effect which will remove any creases. You might like to take this opportunity to iron your clothes instead. Plug in your laptop, set up your cell phone charger, set your alarm and pull out the documents or reading for the next day. By having the same routine each time, you will be productive and not forget important details (and you save time in the morning also).

**Call a client** – You often have down time in the airport, so it is a great time to reconnect with a client or colleague. Use this time to touch base with important people in your life and it becomes part of your business development time, too.

**Be strategic** – Time in hotel rooms can be lonely or unproductive, so use this time to design new products, review business plans, catch-up on reading and design new models or programs for your business. Some of your best ideas might come while sitting in your hotel room – use this time for strategy and thought space instead of turning on the television to keep you company.

**Stay connected** – When you arrive at your location, notify someone important to you. I call my husband when I've arrived so he knows I am safe and sound – and I like to hear his voice. Calling your family or a friend is a great way for you to keep connected on the road.

**Write thank you notes** – We carry stamped stationery when travelling, using the flight home to write notes to people we meet during our trip. When arriving at my next destination, I post them. It is a great way to reconnect with people after you have met them and is a productive use of flight time.

**Exercise** – If you don't have a gym in the hotel consider either taking a walk outside at the beginning of your day or exercising in your room. Place a towel the floor and then do a series of stretches, yoga, sit-ups and pushups. You can establish a routine especially for travel that doesn't require any equipment, i.e., pushups, sit-ups, squats and any yoga.

Here are some ways to make exercise more interesting and not negotiable while you travel:

**Read on the treadmill** – While you won't be working at your maximum intensity, this is multi-tasking. It is astounding how much reading you can achieve while walking on the treadmill. Now some would argue that you are not working hard enough if reading and walking … to them I say – at least I am walking!

**Don't book dinner plans until you have worked out** – Use connecting with someone for dinner as your reward, not as an excuse to avoid exercise.

**Schedule a walk or workout with someone else** – Now this isn't the most glamorous way to meet someone but it is effective. When living in Australia the legendary speaker, Patricia Fripp came to town; I was keen to learn from her, and so we would meet for walks around Sydney Harbor and chat while walking – very productive and healthy too.

**Pack gear** – Not just workout clothing, workout gear. This could include a jump rope, stretch band or yoga DVD to play in your room.

**Load apps** – Find your favorite apps to work out with and install them on your iPad or iPhone. While attending a National Speakers Association event I noticed a speaker friend had P90x loaded on his iPad; he was using it in the gym – great idea.

**Don't turn on the TV** until you … exercise, call a client, unpack and review your presentation – whatever you need to do. Avoid the TV in your hotel room until everything is complete.

**Pack in chunks** - Eliz Greene, healthy heart spokesperson and speaker shared an exercise travel tip to get in two to three chunks of exercise (10 to 15 minutes in duration) to keep your commitment to your health. A quick walk in the morning around the hotel halls, another at lunch and before bed will keep you on track and your heart healthy on the road. Taking a walk outside can also clear your head and help digest information from your meetings. If you are sightseeing choose walking tours. Pay attention to the weather so you don't overheat and drink plenty of water!

## After Your Travel

**Know the quickest route home** – Understand the quickest and least traffic congested way to get out of the airport so you can be home with those you care for in the smallest amount of time. Where we live there are two major ways home and if you take the wrong one at some particular times during the day it can add up to an hour to your ride home (not so much fun after a long flight), so know which ways are best at different times during the day.

**Unpack quickly** – If you arrive home early enough, unpack your bag, refill any necessary toiletry items and allocate clothes for washing or dry cleaning.

**Refill and replace** – Update any items in your pre-packed toiletries or luggage that need attention to save you time for future trips. Note any additional items you may have forgotten on this trip and place them in your luggage so you don't forget them next time.

**Debrief your trip** – Recall any items you missed, notice things that you enjoyed or frustrated you and make the changes that are within your control. Each time you travel you may learn something new that will help you save time or save you frustration for your next travel experience.

**Thank your team** – If you have an assistant, let them know what went well about the trip and any enhancements you would like to make for your next trip. Thank your travel team for the trip planning and also let them know if something didn't go well and discuss how to fix it for the next trip. Thank your client for the opportunity to work with them. If you experienced great service at some point in the trip take the time to email or write a thank you note to that organization. The simple art of thanking people is often overlooked, but is one of the most powerful things you can do and makes someone else's day!

**Gather receipts** – There is so much paperwork collected on trips including boarding passes, rental agreements and food and hotel receipts. Keep this in a central place when you travel (take a clear plastic folder for this very purpose each time you travel). When you arrive home, quickly sort through the paper, action business cards and file any receipts or keep them aside for your clients. Process all your paper within 24 hours.

**Action business cards** – If you have met new people during your business trip, take the time to now action those cards. You might like to write a "nice to meet you" note, scan them and add them to your database and write a note for any follow-up action required. Following this process diligently each time you travel will avoid piles of business cards gathering on your desk (reminding you of action you haven't taken)!

**Be grateful** – If you are travelling for business, it means you have a successful job that is supporting you and your family. Stop hating it and start enjoying it. Giving thanks for the opportunity to see new places, meet new people and share your experience is a privilege.

**Change your language** around travel; enjoy it, embrace it and you will be more productive! Next time you see another road warrior smile at them and let them know you understand. You can be more productive every time you travel by applying these before, during and after you travel strategies.

## Safety systems when you travel

As a productive road warrior we also want you to be safe and develop systems you can use so we interviewed Carol Fredrickson, CEO of Violence Free to provide us with some tips for busy executives.

**Choose luggage tags** – Avoid the laminated tags made from business cards that show your company name, your name and your position. Instead use covered luggage tags, keeping your personal information private.

**Update personal profiles** – For hotels you frequent for business make a note to advise them if you are traveling alone and advise under no circumstances are additional keys to be provided to anyone.

**Ask for non-adjoining rooms** – Unless you really need it.

**Room requests** – Ensure the hotel doesn't assign you to a room at the end of a long hallway near the stairwell; if they do, ask them to reassign a room for you.

We would add to Carol's great suggestions a few additional considerations, especially for women traveling alone:

**Don't give out your room number** – regardless of whom you are with always keep this information private.

**Be aware in the elevator** – Allow other guests to enter their floor number before you enter your own – especially if there are only two of you in the elevator.

**Don't drink in the bar alone** – We consciously choose room service rather than hotel lobby bars to avoid any unnecessary attention or conversation.

**Use valet parking** – Where possible always use the valet service so the staff brings your car to you instead of you being alone in parking garages at night.

## action plan

Who is someone you admire that demonstrates exceptional systems? Write their name here:

_____

Make an appointment to interview them for 15 minutes by phone.
**Ask them, "What systems do you use in your personal and professional life?"**

Write their responses here: _____

_____

_____

_____

_____

_____

_____

_____

_____

_____

Now what will you do differently as a result of reading this chapter?

_____

_____

_____

_____

_____

_____

_____

_____

_____

- **Be clear.**
- **Keep your word, or lose credibility.**
- **Concentrate on long-term goals and focus on short-term results.**
- **Major impact is affected by minor decisions.**
- **Ask yourself three questions.**
- **Prioritize prioritizing.**
- **Structure your week.**
- **Use goals as your filter.**
- **Focus on five.**
- **Schedule YOU first.**
- **Manage interruptions.**
- **Chunk in time blocks for projects.**
- **Delete often.**
- **Create a paperless environment.**
- **Work life balance is a myth – work-life integration is key.**
- **Choose amazing.**
- **Give up the guilt.**
- **Decide your mindset.**
- **Find fabulousness.**
- **Perfection kills productivity.**
- **Choose active abundance.**
- **Done is better than perfect.**

"Energy is the essence of life. Every day you decide how you are going to use it by knowing what you want and what it takes to reach that goal, and by maintaining focus."

- Oprah Winfrey

Filter is a verb meaning to pass (a liquid, gas, light or sound) through a device to remove unwanted material. In Folding Time, filtering means removing unwanted activities and tasks so you can focus on the highest-return activities and results.

A synonym: verb: strain, percolate, filtrate, infiltrate, leach.

I like the word percolate. Often we just jump into our day, jump into a meeting, jump into a conversation without allowing ideas to percolate. When was the last time you percolated?

There is nothing like good Italian coffee. Even if you don't drink a lot of coffee, just one well-made coffee each day using our fabulously flash Italian coffee machine is delicious. As a coffee snob, unfortunately, we can't take our coffee machine on vacation with us; my honey often packs our little Italian percolator to make real coffee on the stovetop. It is a slow old process and we can only make one cup of coffee at a time, but it sure does taste good. It is worth the wait.

Where do you need to percolate your ideas?

Choice is the act of selecting or making a decision when faced with two or more options. When considering filter (or choice) for folding time it is the act of deciding what is the best use of your time, attention and energy – right now!

## Be clear

Be the pioneer: knowing what you want and where you want to be.

Coco Chanel said, "A woman with good shoes is never ugly." She became known for her beige and black shoes – it was a flattering and yet practical design. She was clear about what she wanted for women. She was a fashion pioneer who used jersey fabric in the 1920's for women's clothing (unheard of at the time) because she wanted to create something that was comfortable (also unheard of at the time).

Throughout history there have been many pioneers, including United States' President Barack Obama who became the first black American president in 2008. In June 2010, Julia Gillard became the first female Australian Prime Minister; Margaret Thatcher was the first prime minister in the United Kingdom in 1979. These pioneers were very clear about what they wanted and how they were going to achieve it.

When we are clear about what is important to us, what we want to be known for, and what we want to be remembered for it makes it easier to filter our choices and decide how we are going to invest our time.

## Keep Your Word ... or lose your credibility.

Each day we make choices to honor the commitments we make. When marriage vows are shared in front of people there are words spoken that include love, cherish, honor, respect, promise… these words mean something different to each person.

When we said our marriage vows (over 24+ years ago at the time of this writing) these were words I wanted to keep forever.

Impactful leaders keep their word: they do what they say they will do.

If you want to keep your word, think first. Be conscious of what you agree to do, what you decide to delete and who you decide to donate your time to.

**Take action** – Regardless of how you are feeling, understand the consequences of the decisions you make and honor the commitments you make. Sometimes we don't feel like working out at the gym; however, if you told yourself you would work out to remain strong and healthy for your family and for yourself, then keep your word to yourself.

If you tell your spouse or your kids you will do something and then you don't take action, you damage your relationship with them. When you commit to completing a project for your boss and don't make the deadline, you damage your relationship with them.

If you want to avoid losing credibility – not just with others, but with yourself – you need to filter your decisions to keep your word.

## Concentrate on long-term goals and focus on short-term results

This is a challenge to balance the investment of your time in activities that are both strategic and tactical. When forced with a decision to take action consider the long-term effect of your short-term focus.

### Major impact is affected by minor decisions

Choosing wisely how to invest our time, ability and opportunities in our everyday decisions creates a greater long-term impact.

Every decision could be an important decision. Sometimes the smallest decisions we make don't feel important at the time but the reality of the long-term impact can be huge. We have to weigh up the impact our choices make – not just for today but for a week from now, a month from now, a year from now and so on. Too often in our instant gratification environment we allow others to impact our long-term goals because of their short-term focus.

You can decide to sit down and watch a mindless movie (which I love to do) or you can read a thoughtful book. Sometimes we just want the movie – so do it – however, other times a book is going to have more impact on us. You decide.

Are you hyper-productive before vacation? Do you know what we mean? You have a super-woman (or superman) ability to achieve an enormous amount of completion around tasks you might have been putting off forever: bills get paid, paper gets filed, business cards get entered, calls get returned – all those little jobs you meant to do are completed because you have a hard stop deadline of a vacation. This form of hyper-productive can be useful for extending yourself before you go away – you can have a more relaxing time knowing you don't have a large amount of to-dos waiting for you when you get back. Deciding to work in overdrive (short term) before a vacation can be a good strategy for long-term enjoyment.

As a shoe lover, when originally building my shoe collection I wasn't focused on how long the pairs would last but how many varieties to accumulate. I love choices; I wanted storage space to be able to have many choices regarding shoes. A funny thing happened, I ran out of space! Hard decisions had to be made, who would we would set free, and who could stay. (It is weird I speak of them like personalities.) Now when purchasing shoes, tastes have changed and so has the budget – so I prefer to invest in premium quality shoes that are statement pieces that will last for a long time and not date fashion-wise.

**Ask yourself three questions** – If you want to determine if the project or task you are about to embark on will have an impact, ask yourself these questions:
- ◀ Is this the best use of my time?
- ◀ Is this the best use of my abilities?
- ◀ Is this the best use of my opportunities?

We don't always get it right, but in answering these questions honestly the decisions made have a higher impact.

In the Bible, Matthew 6:19-24 says, "Do not store up for yourselves treasures on earth, where moth and rust destroy, and where thieves break in and steal. But store up for yourselves treasures in heaven, where moth and rust do not break in and steal. For where your treasure is, there your heart will be also."

Regardless of your belief system, the take away in these verses was not really about treasure but about focus.

Where are you focusing your attention, and what decisions are you making?

Could you be more long term focused instead of short term?

Where do you need to focus more on the long term? What short-term activities are jeopardizing the achievement of your long-term goals?

## Prioritize Prioritizing
**You don't have time to do everything;
you only have time to do what matters.**
When was the last time you went on a road trip?

What do you remember from that trip? There is a huge amount of planning that takes place: where to go, what route to take, what to visit, where to stay, what to wear, what snacks to pack on the trip. (No matter which audience I ask this question of, snacks always come up and make me giggle.) Once you have answered all these questions, it is then the time to try and fit it all into the boot of your car (we call it a boot in Australia, in the US it is called the trunk). You have visions of all those suitcases, coolers, snacks and equipment fitting into the boot. My husband is brilliant at this skill; I think boys are born with a packing gene for this very purpose.

Which suitcases do you pack in first?  You don't try and put in all the little things, you always put in the large suitcases first.

Our day is like a road trip. Each day we need to ensure we focus on the large luggage items first. Many people just get little things done so they can cross them off a list; however, this strategy doesn't allow you to have the greatest impact. It makes you feel good in the short term because you think you got something completed, but it doesn't maximize your time.

In Tim Ferris' book *The 4-Hour Work Week,* he shares that he only completes email for one hour per week to allow him to focus on the big items. While this may not be practical for the rest of us who aren't Tim Ferris, I like the idea of just setting a small amount of time aside to complete a task like this. Could you focus on your email for one hour a day? How much more could you achieve?

If you really want to prioritize your day, invest 15 to 30 minutes in the morning to determine your highest priority activities and then focus on the achievement of those.

Influence and communication expert, Stacey Hanke takes this one step further: Stacey **writes her three top priorities every day on a post-it note**. She keeps that post-it note with her until all items are crossed off that list. When she shared this technique with me I started doing it myself, and it really works. That is the best use of post-it notes we have ever seen.

## Use Goals as Your Filter
Know them, keep them present and use as a decision making tool.

In the area where we live, every property has their own well. That's right, a well on my property to source all our water supplies. As a city girl this was very bizarre to me. I grew up with public water and sewage systems. We noticed after living here that our skin and hair felt different and noticed the water needed to be tested and filtered often. It is probably the cleanest water around; however, we are super diligent about changing the filters in our house. If you want quality water… or a quality day, you need to make sure you are filtering.

**Keep goals visual** – Writing down your goals and then posting them in places you can frequently see will also constantly remind you of what is the highest priority. You could post above your desk in your line of sight and also carry them on your iPhone (as a photograph) or carry them in your bag.

**Remove activities from your life** - If you spend several hours cleaning your house on a Saturday morning after working a long week, and you resent every moment of it – it's time to hire a cleaning service. If you spend countless hours in your yard, mowing, weeding and maintaining your garden, maybe it is time to consider a gardening service.

What activities can you remove to help you focus in your goals?

An executive once told me she found that she was working at home – and she didn't mean bringing work home.  She meant she was approaching her home life like she was at work, with an unending list of projects and commitments, and she wasn't enjoying any down time. She changed her priorities so they could be more about prioritizing joy and happiness. Instead of cleaning out her fridge, she chose to go for a drive in the country.  While there comes a time when our fridge does need to be cleaned out, sometimes we need to create a system to allow down time and more joy and happiness.

## Focus on Five - Know why you are doing something

Human beings have been blessed with five senses: sight, smell, sound, taste and touch.  Have you ever met someone who has an incredibly heightened sense of smell? Know anyone who has bionic hearing and can hear a conversation about them when they are in another room?

Some of our senses are more acute than others based on our experiences, upbringing and current events.  Just like we have five senses it is essential to assign goals to five important aspects of your life: spiritual, relational, financial, educational and physical.

Jim Rohan was an American entrepreneur, author and motivational speaker, and a huge influencer in the personal development movement. His books often featured his rags to riches story focusing on attitude and action. I would love to have spent time with Jim, and he was known to say, "We have two choices; we can make a living or design a life."

**Make a date with yourself** – Every January, allocate time in a favorite spot to review the year just past and set goals for your future year. The discipline of this process will ensure you focus on the most impactful activities.

**Set one in five** – Set at least one goal in each of the five areas of spiritual, relational, financial, educational and physical. This discipline ensures you are taking care of your health, the people in your life and the lifestyle you want to lead.

**Joint focus** – If you share your life with someone, consider setting a few joint goals. My husband and I always have joint travel goals so we know where we want to go during the coming year and how to allocate our funding for trips. This might be one of our secrets to being married over 24+ years.

**Daily focus** – When we interviewed Brian Tracy he shared that he writes his goals out daily. Brian is one of the most influential people of our time. Every day he invests in what he calls The Golden Hour: time spent reading his goals, feeding his brain with positive images and visualizing results. He says, "Goals in writing are dreams with deadlines."

## Structure Your Week

Our clients often ask how often asked how to be more productive each day. This is important; however, maybe something even more important to consider is how to be more productive each **week**.

We have a system for our week. Sounds crazy, I know. No week is ever the same; however, you might be surprised that when you create boundaries or structure for your week you can achieve an enormous amount.

As a productivity thought leader, we spend significant time travelling to client sites, walking around convention centres, meeting clients, spending time with women in our mentoring program … oh, and then there is the actual running of the practice, too.

We have found the easiest way to accelerate productivity is to systemize the week. Now like all good systems, we don't get it right every time and it doesn't work every time; however, it is a great guideline for us.

We don't work weekends with clients. We protect weekends as recovery time. We don't fly for clients on weekends (unless they are super special clients); we know this isn't practical for some of you reading this. This is how we try structure our week:

- ◀ Monday – meeting with mentors in the Mentoring Program, networking, client appointments, writing, strategy and often this is a travel day.
- ◀ Tuesday to Thursday – speaking, training, media interviews and travelling.
- ◀ Friday – meeting with mentors, writing, setting up the next week and catch-up.

This simple structure is helpful when we are trying to maximize time balancing what we do with how we do it. Here are some things to consider when building the structure for your week:

**Schedule YOU first** – Book an appointment every day that is focused on you. This might include exercise, mediation, quiet time, reading, self-development – or all of the above!

**Determine what is most important** – What is your plan? What are you working towards? What do you want to achieve? What really lights you up? For me, I love to speak on productivity and to mentor women – simple really. The simplicity allows me to determine where I want to spend my time. It becomes a filtering system for time choices.

**Book administration** – This is not our favorite activity. Even though we have found a way to outsource most of it to our wonderful business manager, Maria Novey, I still have to do some of it myself - we try for Mondays if possible.

**Chunk in time-block for projects** – We all have so many priorities and people wanting our attention. To help structure your week, time-block for projects. For example, co-chairing the UNconference for our professional organization was time intensive and could be a full time job (but wasn't going to increase revenue), so we restricted the times worked on this project to Monday afternoons and Friday mornings.

This simple time-blocking ensured that if we needed to speak with someone, Skype with our co-chair (the fabulous *Getting Geeky* Gina Schreck) or record videos – we did it in one of these time-blocks.

What projects are you working on that you could time-block this week?

**Manage interruptions** – If you work in an office or firm you will find that people are a constant source of interruption (especially your boss!). To help manage these so you can focus on projects and work achievements, consider wearing headphones while you get tasks completed, standing up when someone comes in your office to help accelerate the conversation or creating a do-not-disturb sign (that the whole team understands) while you try and get things done.

## Interruptions can kill your best time-blocking intentions!

**Schedule a trial** – Decide which week you want to try this new strategy. Select a week, advise your team of what you are trying to achieve, schedule your daily appointment and see if it works for you.

This is a system we use and it helps us to keep boundaries with our personal and professional time, and schedule meetings. It also allows me to leverage my travel and to feel more productive each week. Try it and let us know your results.

## Delete Often
### Productivity is about deletion ... not addition

Some of the most productive people I know do less, not more.

Rory Vaden is a self-discipline expert and in his book *Take the Stairs* he states, "The most important skill for the next generation of knowledge worker is not learning what to do but rather determining what not to do."

Increasing productivity requires clear identification of what activities to delete – not to do!

Too often we think we need to add to our to-do list; however, what if you replaced your to-do list with **a to-delete list**?

What activities do you do out of habit?

What if you stopped doing an activity?

What would the impact be?

Do an experiment to see which habits are helping you and which ones are hindering you.

Take action to choose to delete at least two activities today.

We tried an experiment based on a recommendation by an idea in the area of execution thought leader, Peter Cook. Pete suggested that to stay focused while he was writing a book, he would only check social media sites on his iPad. This conscious decision to stop what he was doing on his computer and move to the iPad was a deliberate action.

We tried it and realized how often we would just pop over to HootSuite or Facebook to review, read, procrastinate and waste time enjoying other people's lives – instead of focusing on the completion of the task or project that was a much higher priority. This simple but effective change in my habit saved me an enormous amount of time – thanks, Pete!

One of the interior decorators in our Mentoring Program shared with us that before she could make over a room for a client, she totally removed all items in the space so she could start afresh. She then had a clean slate to create, and by deleting and sorting items this helped the clients also enjoy their spaces more.

Personal organizers can be hired to come into your space and help you systemize. The first step is to **delete and remove the clutter** that can create overwhelm. Where in your life do you need to do more deleting instead of more doing?

## Use the delete key

Before changing over from a PC to a Mac I was fascinated with the keys that were truly well worn. The delete key on the keyboard was hard to read and it made me smile – oh, how I love the delete key! So often we are scared to delete that email or not respond when it could be the best use of our time and most appropriate response.

Can you wear out your delete key?

**Don't return email** – You don't need to reply to every single email you receive. You can simply press the delete key. I dare you. See what happens. At least 20% of your inbox does not require you to respond. Check your inbox and see if this is correct.

**Remove clutter.** Cluttered or messy areas at home or at work can feel out of control. The clutter is a constant reminder of things you need to do, and it can make us feel overwhelmed and out of balance. Take time to sort the clutter. You don't have to tackle everything at once; make an appointment with yourself to spend just 15 minutes each week improving a different area in your environment. You may want to make this a high priority at the office. Many people believe that a cluttered desk is the sign of a cluttered mind which is not the impression you want to give your colleagues. If your home is cluttered you may want to seek the services of a professional to help you get organized, or you could recruit a friend and make a day of it.

Career Builder did a survey that found 28% of supervisors are less inclined to promote someone with a not-so-neat workspace – I guess many people believe a cluttered desk is the sign of a cluttered mind. A Dutch study challenged this when experts from University of Groningen in the Netherlands revealed that having an office in disarray can actually help people perform better. "Clutter activates the need for organization and clear thinking," says lead author Jia Liu Ph. D, who continues on to say that it can even make a co-worker sitting in the next cubicle more productive. It is rumored that even Albert Einstein worked in a chaotic environment, and he was able to create all kinds of brilliance (not sure that would work for me)!

**Create a paperless desk** – It is not a myth; it can be your reality! Consider keeping your desk clear for only work you are focused on right now. Before you move onto another task can you take action or file the document you are working on? Establish files for projects, reference folders for information you need to access regularly, a reading file for miscellaneous articles and journals and a daily file for administrative activities – keep these documents off your desk – use drawers or shelving.

Out of sight, out of mind – remove that old in-tray you have sitting on your desk. Keep it out of sight.

## Work/Life Balance is a big fat Myth – Integration leaves a legacy

The word *balance* conjures up images of scales where the two sides must be equal in order to be in balance. I don't believe in work/life balance. It's not possible for most people to spend an equal amount of time at work and at play; however, you can create a combination that works for you and in doing so enjoy a lifestyle that gives you whatever it is that you need in your work and your life.

A better description of this concept is work/life integration. Rather than trying to achieve an impossible or precarious balance, integration is about mixing, combining, assimilating, adding and amalgamating – it's about finding the right combination of work and play for you. And what that means is that work/life integration is going to look very different for different people – it all depends on your wants, needs, goals and life circumstances. Of course they are constantly changing, so achieving effective integration requires your ongoing focus. Unfortunately there's no magic formula or prescription for achieving work/life integration, but with the right guidance and tools you'll be well on the way to identifying what works best for you.

Begin by getting those images of balance out of your mind, and let's start time with a triangle of three equal sides. The first side represents your emotions, the second represents your expectations and the third is your environment. When each of these aspects of your life is working well, you achieve work/life integration.

emotions · expectations · environment

## Are you achieving integration in your life?

It's relatively easy to tell whether we're living a well-integrated life or not: it's simply the way we feel. If you feel that your life is on track, if you are happy, if your environment is satisfying, if your relationships are working well and your health is good – you have achieved integration. Likewise, if you feel that some areas of your life are not what you would like them to be, it may be time to reassess and make some changes. You can begin by asking yourself some key questions:

**What is important to you?** This is not an easy question to answer. Make an appointment with yourself to sit down somewhere quiet and list the things that are really important to you. Your list might include:

- ◀ Paying off your mortgage.
- ◀ Spending quality time with your family.
- ◀ Taking that trip to Italy that you've been putting off for years.
- ◀ Paying for your child's education.
- ◀ Finally buying that Gucci bag you've always wanted.
- ◀ Spending time with your grandchildren.
- ◀ Learning to paint.
- ◀ Saving money for home remodeling.

**How will you achieve it?** When you have your list, review and see if there are some items that need your attention. When you know what is important to you, you can make more effective choices about how you should be spending your time by asking, "What activities and tasks will help me to achieve the things I want?"

Keep your list of priorities handy and refer to it regularly to help keep you on track when it comes to deciding how to spend your time.

**What are you prepared to give up?** Sometimes achieving integration means giving up activities, tasks, obligations and pleasures in order to get what you really want.

If making additional money is important to you in the short term, you may decide to spend more time at work, take on extras shifts, work public holidays, get a second job or do whatever you need to do to make extra money. And while it may seem that other activities are being neglected, that's OK as long as you have consciously chosen to place earning money as a higher priority than other things in the short term. Likewise, if getting healthy is important to you, you may find that you need to sacrifice certain social events, watch what you eat, spend more time at the gym or get up earlier so that you have more time to exercise, but again, these will be conscious choices about how you spend your time that will help you to achieve the things that are most important to you.

So even though we're no longer aiming for balance, integration still requires us to make choices about what we do and don't want, about what's important and about what we're prepared to give up in order to get more of the things we really want in our lives.

## What is not negotiable?

We all have obligations, activities and tasks that we can't possibly give up, but there are also many that we could let go. Make a list of what really is not negotiable in your life to help you determine what you can change or negotiate in your daily or weekly schedule. Your list might include:

◀ A weekly date night with your partner.
◀ Visiting an elderly relative every Sunday afternoon.
◀ Attending your Saturday morning yoga class.
◀ Watching your daughter's weekly karate class.

Your responses to these questions will begin to guide you as to how to spend your time in order to live the life you desire. Now, let's look at the different aspects of our work/life integration triangle a little more closely and identify some tips and strategies to help you get each of the sides working well.

## Your emotions

The first side of our triangle represents emotions. Sometimes it's not our circumstances but our emotions that can make us feel that life is out of balance, and the scenarios that we create in our own heads are often far worse and far more stressful than what's really going on in our lives.

We need to recognize our emotions, understand where they are coming from and start managing them so that they don't end up managing us.

**Give up guilt.** Guilt is a negative emotion that is not good for either your body or your mind.

Many of us feel guilty because we spend so much time working in our jobs that our household chores don't get completed. We see the laundry piling up, the dishes in the sink, the ironing that never gets done and the yard work that is incomplete. This can make us feel inadequate about our ability to run a household and guilty because we believe our homes must be perfectly clean, tidy and well-presented 100 percent of the time. Many of us would prefer to be working than doing domestic tasks – and we feel guilty about that, too!

**Stop feeling guilty for not 'getting everything done'** and start realizing how much you are achieving. Then, do something about it. For example, you could outsource your cleaning to a service, pay a neighbor to help you or get your family involved in sharing the household chores.

Look around you and ask yourself: what is making you feel guilty? Then, make a plan to deal with the situation (or your perception of it) and eliminate the guilt.

**Choose your mood.** If you are beginning to have a sense of being overwhelmed in your work or family life, choose to remain calm. It can be as simple as that: just tell your mind and your heart to remain calm. You can make a conscious effort to choose your mood each day. Don't let your circumstances or other people determine your state of mind – you choose.

**Plan down time**. Relaxation is crucial for all human beings – it's not negotiable. So make time (schedule it in your calendar) and find ways to relax. If relaxing is something new to you, you might need to make a list of those things that you enjoy doing and find relaxing until they become more familiar to you.  By including some of these activities in your daily schedule, you'll always have something to look forward to, no matter how busy your life gets. Here are a few suggestions to get you started:

- ◀ Walk around your neighborhood.
- ◀ Watch an old movie.
- ◀ Take a bubble bath.
- ◀ Pick fresh flowers from the market.
- ◀ Get a massage.
- ◀ Burn a candle.
- ◀ Meditate.
- ◀ Bake cookies.
- ◀ Play Frisbee in the park with a friend.
- ◀ Walk on the beach.
- ◀ Play with a pet.

**Book vacations in advance.**  Vacations give your body and mind an opportunity to relax and recharge – and they give you something wonderful to look forward to. Booking your vacations in advance means that you have to schedule activities around them which is so much easier than trying to plan a break in the middle of a busy year. You'll never have the excuse of not having enough time again.  Plan to invest a minimum of two weeks' vacation every year.

**Enjoy the moment.**  Take time every day to simply stop, look around and enjoy the moment, whatever you are doing.  We all have things to be immensely grateful for in our lives; don't forget to acknowledge and enjoy them along the way.

**Energize yourself.** We're always being told to "take time out for ourselves" but for many people, women in particular, it just seems too difficult. Often, when they do take time out, they feel guilty or selfish. It's time to get over it and learn to take time out each week to do something that energizes you – it might be a yoga class, painting in a studio, putting on headphones and getting lost in the music – whatever it is, find activities that energize you and make appointments with yourself to enjoy them each week

## Your expectations

The second side of our work-life integration triangle represents our expectations. Sometimes feelings of being out of control arise simply because we don't set clear expectations for others or ourselves. Be aware of other people's expectations of you and help to adjust them where necessary by setting realistic timeframes, using language that doesn't include stress or urgency and explaining things calmly. Try applying some of these strategies to ensure that everyone's expectations are managed and realized.

**Communicate**. Ask. It can be as simple as that. Ask others what their expectations are and listen to their responses. Also, let them know what your expectations are and check that they understand them clearly. Most misunderstandings around expectations can be resolved simply by better communication – so listen, restate and repeat.

**Set achievable goals.** If you like setting goals and writing them down, you may find that you sometimes put unrealistic pressure on yourself by making them too difficult or not allowing enough time to achieve them – and that's added stress that you can really do without. It is important to challenge yourself and strive to achieve the things you want in your life, but not if it just stresses you out and makes you unhappy! Take a moment to review your goals and determine if they are the right ones for you at this time.

**Be realistic.** Stop overbooking your schedule. Allow yourself enough time for tasks, rethink your deadlines and stop overcommitting yourself. Underestimating the amount of time it takes to complete a task can be the cause of much frustration. We all tend to underestimate the amount of time things will take and overestimate what we're able to achieve. Learn to allow realistic timeframes for all your activities, and you'll be taking a lot of pressure off yourself.

**Schedule routine.** Make a note of all your regular and routine commitments in your calendar so that you know you cannot give that time to anyone else – it helps stop double-booking time. Book time for regular appointments including haircuts, dentist appointments, family appointments and time for meals. (Yes, you do need to eat properly every day, this is not negotiable.) Whatever regular activity or routine you have in your life – schedule it. And don't forget to schedule travel time to get you to and from your appointments also.

**Avoid sharing**. While we're talking about scheduling, if you work in a team environment where other people have access to your calendar, block out chunks of time in which you can actually get work done, and don't allow others to make appointments in your schedule without your permission. You might need to make the same arrangements in your family life if your partner or other family members are constantly making commitments with your time – set some rules and block out time for yourself.

**Watch your language.** Stop using words like urgent and ASAP. It seems like everything is urgent, and remember that ASAP means "as soon as possible", not right now! As soon as possible might be next week. This language of urgency only increases your stress level and causes frustration to you and others when it results in rushed deadlines or over-commitment so avoid using them.

**Avoid crazy deadlines**. Where possible, plan your time so that you're not doing crazy things to meet crazy deadlines. While it's sometimes necessary, it's no way to work on an ongoing basis, and it'll only lead to stress, worry and, potentially, illness.

**Plan recovery time.** If you know that you have a huge deadline or big event coming up that you'll be working hard to complete, book some time in with yourself for the day after to recover. Plan this time as if it were any other non-negotiable appointment. This is especially important for high achievers who work at high levels for long periods of time and then crash after a big project or deadline - and bounce back to do it all again after they have recovered. It's not for everyone, but it's how some people operate, and for them recovery is especially important.

**Accept the seasons**. We are all used to having four distinct seasons each year. We don't question it when winter comes around (whether we like it or not) – achieving work/life integration is much the same. We need to accept that there are seasons in our lives and that some may seem more extreme than others. There may be times when we need to work harder to achieve more and to take advantage of opportunities, and other times when things are slower, we have more time to relax and enjoy our surroundings. Whatever is happening in your life, accept that it is just the season and in time it will change.

## Your Environment

The third side of our work/life integration triangle represents our environment. Our environment can play a huge rule in determining our emotions and expectations. If it is out of control we can feel overwhelmed, frustrated and angry; if it is in balance we feel more content and happy. Look around you; what effect are your surroundings having on you? Use some of these strategies to make sure that your environment is a positive one that has a good effect on you and everyone else that comes into it.

**Surround yourself with positivity.** Help create your positive emotional state by having photos, pictures, motivational posters and quotes that inspire you in your work and home environment.

**Use your senses.** Surround yourself with items that will improve your environment. This might include scented candles, aromatherapy oils, relaxing music, even a water feature. You'll be more productive and happier in your environment if it has pleasant sounds, smells and visuals.

As our lives go through different seasons, this has been a good one for me. It allowed me to slow down, take stock and enjoy my surroundings and this new adventure. Thankfully, it didn't take a crisis or major life incident to make my husband and I reassess our work/life integration, we just moved countries!

Change is a great thing. I have embraced it, immersed myself in it and surrounded myself with wonderful people who make each day more memorable and rewarding.

Maybe the concept of balance is a big fat myth, but the key to making it work for you is absolutely learning to integrate your emotions, your expectations and your environments.

## Decide your Mindset

Stephen Covey, author of *First Things First,* has a personal philosophy of live, love, learn and leave a legacy. In his book he said, "Basing our happiness on our ability to control everything is futile." He is right! We can't control everything that happens in our lives; however, we can choose our response to the situation.

Folding Time is a mindset that requires you to consider how you invest your time, attention and energy.

The combination of accountability, engagement and leverage ensures that we have created a mindset that will help us conquer each and every day.

## Choose Amazing

The word amazing is an adjective meaning startlingly impressive! Don't you love that explanation? To be amazing takes a daily choice to live an impactful life with great results.

**Make a list of amazing** – What are you grateful for? If you have days when you aren't feeling like you are enjoying where you are at, make a list of everything you are grateful for – this list will help you to filter your mood to change your focus.

**Create an attitude to-do list** – Many years ago I created an attitude to-do list. It contained a list of things that could be done to change my own attitude and impact the people around me. Each day I try to achieve one or more items on it such as:

◀ Smile at every person I meet
◀ Mentally list 10 things I'm grateful for before I climb out of bed
◀ Send a hand written note to remind someone how much I appreciate them
◀ Leave a voicemail for someone reminding them I thought of them today
◀ Sending a fun text to a friend
◀ Giving a referral

These small activities can have significant impact on the person receiving them. What would go on your attitude to-do list?

## Choose Active Abundance

To have abundance is to have a very large quantity of something. Abundant thinking is often associated with positive thinking. I like to think it also means knowing there is enough for everyone; enough business, enough opportunities, enough friendships, enough time. We are all gifted the same amount of time each day.

In Chris Anderson's book *Free*, he challenges readers to embrace a gift economy and shares that, "Today's knowledge workers are yesterday's factory workers."

Knowledge is in abundance, and we need to share that knowledge with those around us. It is readily available and free for most.

While information and knowledge is in abundance, we have to make conscious choices about how to share this and what to abandon.

Productivity is often about deciding what not to pursue, rather than trying to pursue everything.  One of our biggest challenges is making that choice when there are so many available to us.

In *Free,* Anderson continues, "Abundance thinking is not only discovering what will become cheaper but looking for that will be more valuable as a result of moving to that."

Time has become more valuable! We need an abundance mentality of how we can invest our time more wisely, with people we enjoy more, doing things we enjoy more; we want to filter our daily decisions to choose the most impactful activities.

To choose more abundance you can try these strategies:

**Decline invitations that don't excite you** – When you receive a request from someone to attend something you aren't super excited about or delighted to attend, graciously decline their invitation. Save your time for things that energize you.

**Fully commit** – If you are working on a project give it your all. If you are in a conversation give it your whole heart. If you are relaxing with a book fully immerse yourself in it. Choose that you will fully commit to the person, the project or the time allocation.

**Be generous** – When you are able to share your time with others, make it a priority to remain undistracted. When you share a meal with someone cover the costs. When you drive through a tollgate pay for the car behind you. (It is funny to watch their faces in your rear view mirror!) When you buy flowers for your client grab an extra bunch for someone you care about.

Abundant thinking includes knowing how to share your time, attention and energy with those around you. What can you to do today so abundance wins and you increase your daily impact?

## Find Fabulousness

Fabulousness is a daily state of mind. It is more than a fun word. It is one of my daily mantras.

The word *fabulous* is believed to have originated in the 15th century where mythical creatures were featured in fables. From fables comes the adjective that means extraordinary: extraordinarily large, amazingly good and/or wonderful. This means we can choose this state of mind.

Ask yourself the question, "How can I make this more fabulous?" This is a way to approach projects, meetings, events and conversations. How can you make it more memorable, impactful, fun or entertaining?

In Sally Hogshead's book *Fascinate* she shares that, "When it comes to staying fit, the fear of looking unattractive is more motivating that the hope of a slim physique." This comment got me thinking. Is that true?

A quick, informal survey of girlfriends found she was absolutely right! It wasn't always the health benefits or increased energy that drove people to stay fit … they wanted to look fabulous! Vanity wins!

**De-clutter draining Distractions** – Eliminate mental, physical and emotional distractions.

Have you ever sorted your shoe collection?

For some of you this may not be an issue. Those of you who know me you know my shoe collection is a source of joy for me.

One day when I realized that there wasn't an option of adding any more friends to my collection, I took out every pair and laid them on the floor (it took up the entire space of the floor). I am embarrassed to say there were pairs I had forgotten about, pairs I had never worn and pairs that had been worn so much it was time to retire them.

These were more than shoes to me, these were friends who had helped me create special memories, been on stage when I had received an award, tracked through a favorite holiday destination, represented a conference I organized – there were memories in each pair. The simple act of choosing who got to go back into the shoe wardrobe and who got set free wasn't an easy task for me. There was too much emotional attachment to them and not enough physical space to store them. I did consider asking my honey to build a whole new room for them … but I decided against that – remember, I want to remain married.

My shoe clutter had become a distraction, and so I spent hours sorting, cleaning and storing them again. It was an interesting experiment as I realized others would benefit more from my collection than me, and I happily donated several bags of shoes to many sources. What remained were my absolute favorites.

**Emotional** – Guilt is a powerful chemical caused by higher concentrations of cortisol and noradrenaline (stress hormones) that occurs in the brain and causes us to waste time and energy on conversations or situations that don't increase our productivity. Eliminate guilt: embrace gratefulness.

**Physical** – Look around you. Does your environment distract you because of the clutter? Time to take action. Clean: file, action, throw away. Whatever you have to do to eliminate the distractions around you – do it!

**Mental** – Distractions caused by social media and email may cost a 1,000 worker company more than $10 million a year says a survey published in *USA Today* (5/19/2011). We need to focus our mental energy by investing time. A regular brain dump can help eliminate the distractions floating around in your brain.

One of my dear friends knows that when things are feeling overwhelming she grabs her label maker and starts to organize and eliminate clutter. It has become a joke between us that when she reaches for her label maker you know life has become overwhelming.

## Perfection kills productivity – 80% is OK

Several of our clients share that they want everything to be perfect. Voltaire once said, "The perfect is the enemy of the good." He's right; the challenge with perfection is that it kills productivity.

Perfection is selfishly keeping your brilliance to yourself, and that doesn't help the world.

As mentioned earlier, Pareto, the Italian economist who discovered in 1906 that 80% of the landmass in Italy was owned by only 20% of the population. He also later discovered that 20% of the pea pods in his garden contained 80% of the peas!

This became known as the Pareto principle – or 80/20 rule – and is sometimes referred to as The Law of the Vital Few. It states that for many events, roughly 80% of the effect comes from 20% of the causes.

Regardless of how you apply this rule, it works. For example, we women wear 20% of our wardrobe 80% of the time (but don't share this with your partner); we receive 80% of our revenue from 20% of our clients. This rule has another use: I think it is better to have 80% of an idea out in the world than 100% and still in your head!

**It is OK not to be perfect**. I am not saying only 80% quality – you still need to spell check and provide value; however, seeking 100% on all activities and tasks in your life gets in the way of execution. Choose that 80% is OK.

## Done is better than perfect.

Perfection kills productivity but execution creates momentum.

Rory Vaden in his book *Take the Stairs* shares that, "Action is the inevitable pre-requisite for our success." So true!

**Do something** - If you constantly wait to make something perfect, the world won't see it. If you don't have time to type a letter send a handwritten note;  people will appreciate you thought of them. If you really want to write a book chapter but don't know where to start write a blog post first. Get it out there.

**Create public deadlines** - If you have wanted to create a public workshop to attract new clients and add value to your existing clients, consider posting the date, booking the venue, sending the invitation, allowing guests to register  and THEN finalize the content of the workshop. I have created product offer order forms before products have been finished and it motivates me to get them complete.  We are so driven to keep our word that this public declaration will force you to complete it.

### Spotlight on Joan Walsh, founder of Kashbox Coaching.

You will often hear people around you say, "There are never enough hours in the day" or "I don't have time." These are not phrases you will hear from executive coach, author and co-founder of Kashbox Coaching,  Joan Walsh.

While researching this book we interviewed Joan about her incredible ability to make impactful decisions daily.  Joan is a walking miracle; in 2010 Joan had a brain aneurysm … 15 months after this event she was addressing a room full of women leaders accepting the Female Business Leader of the Year award for the impact she had made on the business community. Joan is highly productive, and she attributes that to her ability to make the right choices daily.

Before Joan's illness she was an extremely hard working perfectionist with a full calendar of coaching clients and speaking engagements. Constantly traveling, contributing to her community, Alumni and family, she took care of her health - she was one of the hardest working women I knew. It took an illness to finally slow her down.

Here is a summary of our conversation to help all busy leaders prioritize themselves and filter decisions to have a great impact on those around them:

**Plan each day ... the day before** – We say, plan tomorrow today. Joan practices this by reviewing her calendar, making her to-do list and leveraging her most energetic time.

**Event management** – Keep a close watch on your energy; be OK with cancelling attendance or rescheduling an event based on your energy levels. Consider attending part of an event but not the whole event if you need to.

**Rest daily** – While we aren't advocating you take a nap at your desk (but wouldn't this be a treat some days), Joan makes rest a priority in her afternoon schedule to continue to be productive throughout the day. Maybe you could take a power nap.

**Prioritize your top 10** – Each month determine the top 10 priorities to achieve that month and then make your decisions based on those priorities. This helps you stay focused and avoids distraction.

**Invest 30 minutes daily to review** – We advocate 15 minutes each morning to identify your top three strategic activities for the day and then 10 at night to plan tomorrow today. Joan shared that she does this to make sure she is focused and applying her energy to the right priorities.

Interestingly, since Joan's illness she chooses to only work in the mornings each day. She has structured her business for client appointments in the morning and rest and recovery in the afternoon. During her afternoons she does research, reads, updates herself on industry events and is very strategic. As her energy is highest in the morning she is taking this time to do what is best for her. Could you apply a similar strategy when controlling your calendar? Choose your most productive time and schedule your interactions during this time.

Joan will tell you her illness is one of the best things to happen to her and her family. She was forced to filter her choices daily based on her energy and what was truly important to her.

Don't wait until you get sick or lose someone you love to reassess your priorities. Take action today to filter your choices for maximum impact.

Choose **blissful productivity** – In *Aspire*, Kevin Hall shares that mythologist Joseph Campbell coined the phrase, "Follow your bliss."

Every day you get an opportunity to **filter multiple choices** - use your values and goals to help you choose your highest priorities to determine which tasks or activities you need to invest in.

Who is someone you admire that demonstrates an exceptional ability to make good choices?
Write their name here:

_____

## action plan

Make an appointment to interview them for 15 minutes by phone.
**Ask them, "How do you make such good choices in your personal and professional life?"**

Write their responses here: _____

_____

_____

_____

Now what will you do differently as a result of reading this chapter? _____

_____

_____

_____

# "Great acts are made up of small deeds."

- Lao Tzu

The secret to Folding Time … is to do something, anything! Don't just sit there thinking about what you read and what that means to you – do something, anything!

Folding Time is about being accountable for our time, engaging our attention and leveraging our energy. When you combine these vital success filters you are able to ensure that every project you invest in you can approach with full integrity, and you will have an impact on the planet.

Don't wait.

Take action.

Do something now.

People that talk about doing things but never get around to it are not Folding Time. They are wasting time. Don't be that person.

Choose to take action on what you have read.

Choose to dial down your stress. Allow yourself time.

Most people want a secret formula, a short cut (like a crash diet). There isn't a crash diet or secret formula or magic pill for Folding Time.

It is all about the choices you make.

**Choose to take action today.**

**action plan**

Who is your accoutability partner?  Write their name here:

_____

Write the name of someone you admire who demonstrates the characteristics of Folding Time:

_____

# Set up a time to interview them and learn their secrets.

Write their responses here: _____

_____

_____

_____

_____

_____

Let's build your Folding Time action plan today.  Insert your action items from each chapter on the next page so you have one total action plan.

# Folding Time Action Plan

| Folding Time | Activity | Due Date |
|---|---|---|
| **Accountability** | | |
| **Engagement** | | |
| **Leverage** | | |
| **Filter** | | |
| **Flow** | | |

# Folding Time Action Plan

| Reward for Achievement | What will get in your way of achieving this? |
|---|---|
| | |
| | |
| | |
| | |
| | |

# about neen james

Neen James, MBA CSP, is the CEO of Neen James Communications and she is obsessed with productivity!

From the board room to the meeting table, leaders, employees and entrepreneurs alike relate immediately to Neen's candid, engaging delivery on a variety of topics like: productivity and productive presentation skills.

An international productivity thought leader and native born Aussie, Neen is best known for her engaging keynotes that have educated, entertained and yes, charmed audiences with real-world strategies that apply in all roles, whether at work or in life.

With a solid background in learning and development and in managing large teams at various corporations, Neen is a natural fit for organizations looking for presenters that focus on productivity strategies, tools and resources. Clients like Comcast, Cisco, Virgin, Pfizer, FBI and BMW describe Neen as "authentic" and "passionate" with subject matter that is spot on. Neen also provides one-on-one consulting and mentoring on a variety of business topics.

As one of the partners of Thought Leaders Global, Neen loves helping clever people become commercially smart.

Neen is a sought-after media expert providing her views and expertise in publications around the world, including *The Philadelphia Business Journal*, *the Singapore Times*, *Working Woman*, and *MacWorld Magazine*, to name a few. A published author of nine books, including *Folding Time*, *Secrets of Super-Productivity*, *Strategic Networking* and *Network or Perish*, Neen puts substance behind her sass.

Neen earned her MBA from Southern Cross University in Australia. She an active member of the National Speakers Association, and serves on several Boards.

When she isn't working, Neen travels the world collecting fabulous shoes, a fetish she candidly admits to. You may also find Neen traveling the United States on her Harley Davidson motorcycle.

Visit www.neenjames.com for more information on programs and services offered by Neen James.

We can help you personally in your quest to Fold Time.

Maybe you want to move ahead but you are unsure
what the right action plan is for you? Where do you start?

**We can help you with that.**

Maybe you need to incorporate more accountability into your life and you
want to work with a coach who can help you do that. Maybe you want an
accelerated experience and need a mentor to guide you through, or maybe
your team needs a speaker for their annual event to inspire them to take
action and Fold Time at your organization.

Whether you are an individual or an organization
wanting to Fold Time, we can help you.

Please contact our office and our super fabulous team
would be delighted to assist you.

**Neen James**
**Productivity Thought Leader**

Neen James is an international productivity thought leader who delivers
engaging keynotes that have educated and entertained audiences with
real-world strategies that apply in all roles, whether at work or in life.
Neen also provides one-on-one consulting and mentoring and helps
women become commercially smart.

www.neenjames.com

**Other titles by Neen James**

Secrets of Super-Productivity:
How to Achieve Amazing Things in Your Work Life


**Other books and CD programs Neen has contributed to:**

How to Be a Productive Road Warrior

Secrets of Super-Productivity Toolkit for Work and Home

Balance: Real life strategies for Work-life balance

Network or Perish

Strategic Networking

6 Essentials for Success in Business and Life

How to Run a Successful Home Based Business

Thought Leaders Ideas: Volume 3

What My Favorite Teacher Taught Me – Volume 1